Mullā Ṣadrā Shīrazi

On the Hermeneutics of the Light Verse of the Qur'ān
(*Tafsīr Āyat al-Nūr*)

Translated, introduced and annotated by
Latimah-Parvin Peerwani

ICAS Press

Dedicated to my parents
Ṣadr al-Dīn and Sherbanu Peerwani

British Library Cataloguing-in-Publication Data
A catalogue record for this book is available from the
British Library

ISBN 1 904063 16 0

This edition first published 2004

Published by
Islamic College for Advanced Studies Press (ICAS)
133 High Road, Willesden, London NW10 2SW

Contents

Acknowledgements 7
Translator's Introduction 9
Author's Introduction 33

[The First] Chapter 35
God is the Light of the heavens and the earth; the similitude of His Light is that of a lamp in a niche 35
Detailed Reminder 38
Excursion 46
Section 47
Wisdom [Derived from] the Throne 50
Illuminative Flash 52
Assistance through Unveiling 54
Fiery Unveiling 55

[The Second] Chapter 59
The similitude of His Light is that of a lamp in a niche, the lamp is in a glass; the glass is like a glittering star 59
Excursion 62
Admonition 63
Another Way [of Admonition] 65

[The Third] Chapter 69
Kindled from a blessed tree, an olive that is neither of the Orient nor of the Occident 69
The Earthly Shadow in which is the Illumination from the Throne 73
Sacred Section 79
Section 80

Illuminative Unveiling 81
Subtle Point [Derived] from the Throne 83

[The Fourth] Chapter 85
God guides to His light whom He wills 85
Reminder 87
Similitude of the Throne 87
Admonition and Allusion 89
Unveiling of the Spiritual State for the Verification of Discourse 91
Allusion 92
Section 94
Inspirational Subtle Point 98
Enlightening Reminder 98
Guidance 101
Comprehensive Logos 102
[Perfect Man] is Comprehensive Light and Comprehensive Locus of Divine Epiphany 104
Divine Wisdom in Adamic Logos 106
Adamic Mirror which Contains the Signs of the Lord and the Lights of Mercy 108
Illuminations and Allusions 113
Muḥammadan Wisdom 115
Elaboration of Discourse for the Clarification of Station 119
Philosophical Foundation on which the Principles of Gnosis are Based 121
[Divine] Assistance 126
Reminder 128
Admonishing Reminder 131
Banishing Doubt 132

Conclusion and Testament 135

Glossary 143
Bibliography 149
Index of the Qur'ānic Verses 153
Index of Ḥadīths and Sayings 159
Index of Names and Terms 163

Acknowledgements

The librarians Mr Adam Gecek and Miss Salwa Ferahian of the Institute of Islamic Studies, McGill University, Montreal, were most kind in assistance, as were the librarians Mr Alnoor Merchant of the Institute of Ismaili Studies, London, the late Dr Aliya Haji of the al-Furqan Islamic Heritage Foundation of London and the librarians of the School of Oriental and African Studies, London. I should like to thank Professor S. H. Nasr, my former supervisor, for giving his valuable time in going through some pages of the translation and giving his general suggestions for its improvement.

I am most grateful to Mr Hamid Tehrani of the Islamic College for Advanced Studies, London, who not only meticulously edited the manuscript but also collated the translation with the Arabic text and gave useful suggestions, and Mr Khalil Toussi for facilitating the publication of this work.

Mullā Ṣadrā: Foremost Among the Transcendent Philosophers (*Ṣadr al-Muta'allihin*)

A Brief Sketch of His Biography and His Works on the Qur'ān

Ṣadr al-Dīn (or Mullā Ṣadrā as he is known in Iran) was born in Shiraz, Iran, in 979/1571 in a Twelver Shī'ite family. His father, Ibrāhim Shīrāzī, a member of the famous Qawām family of Shiraz, held the post of vizier and was a powerful political and social figure in his native city. He spared no efforts in the education of his only son. The young Ṣadr al-Dīn was given the best possible early Islamic education in Shiraz. After that he was sent to Isfahan to continue his studies.

In this epoch Isfahan was not only the political capital of the Safavid dynasty but also the centre of the scientific life of Iran. Here lived and worked some of the greatest masters of learning, whose teaching extended to a wide field of knowledge. At Isfahan Ṣadr al-Dīn had as principal masters three people who are famous in the history of Islamic thought and spirituality in Iran. The first was Shaykh Bahā' al-Dīn Āmilī (d. 1030/1621), with whom Ṣadrā studied the traditional Islamic transmitted sciences, i.e. the Qur'ān and its science, Ḥadīth of the Prophet and the Shī'ite Imams and its science, Shī'ī jurisprudence and its principles. He studied intellectual sciences with Mīr Dāmād (d. 1041/1631) and Mīr Findiriskī (d. 1050/1640).

Not satisfied with mere formal learning, and also persecuted by many legal Shī'ī scholars for his adherence to philosophy (*ḥikmah*) and gnosis (*'irfān*), Mullā Ṣadrā left worldly life in general and retired to the small market-town of Kahak some thirty kilometres southwest of Qum in north-central, Iran where he is said to have stayed for seven long years or even, according to another report, fifteen years. There he contemplated deeply and sincerely, as he claims in his introduction to his *Asfār*,[1] the fundamental problems relating to the knowledge of God, existence, human destiny, creation, etc. This intense contemplation was accompanied by strenuous religious exercises and discipline based on the Islamic Sharī'ah and the teachings of the Prophet and Shī'ite Imams until, as Ṣadrā claims,[2] he became flooded with insights about these issues. Not only did he rediscover what he had previously learned through rational proofs in a fresh, direct and intuitive way, but also many new truths about the problems he was contemplating dawned upon him. After his years of seclusion he returned once again to the social milieu. Meanwhile, Allāhwirdī Khān, the governor of Shiraz, had built a large *madrasah* (college) in Shiraz and he invited Mullā Ṣadrā to return to his native city and serve in that college as the head teacher. Ṣadrā accepted the offer and taught for many years at the *madrasah* of Khān, which became, thanks to him, the major centre of intellectual sciences in Persia. He led his life according to Islamic Sharī'ah accompanied by spiritual practices, wrote works on metaphysics, metaphysical commentary on several verses and chapters of the Qur'ān, which numbers almost three thousand printed pages, and on the Traditions of the Prophet and Shī'ite Imams.

All his works are in Arabic except for one (*Se Aṣl*), which is Persian, his mother tongue. He trained many students, two of whom later became his sons-in-law, Mullā 'Abd al-Razzāq Lāhijī and Mullā Muḥsin Fayḍ Kāshānī, who are also famous as philosophers in the

---

1. Ṣadr al-Dīn al-Shīrāzī. *Al-Ḥikmat al-Muta'ālīyah fī al-Asfār al-Arba'ah* (*Asfār*), vol. 1, p. 8.
2. *Ibid.*

Shī'ite milieu. Ṣadrā died in Basra, Iraq, while returning from his seventh pilgrimage to Mecca in 1050/1640 and was buried there.[1]

Mullā Ṣadrā wrote four works on the commentary on the Qur'ān:

1. *Mutashābihāt al-Qur'ān* (The Ambiguous or Equivocal Verses of the Qur'ān).[2] This is a short epistle, which deals with some ambiguous verses of the Qur'ān and Ṣadrā's methodology in dealing with such verses.

2. *Asrār al-āyāt* (The Mysteries of the Qur'ānic Verses).[3] In this work Ṣadrā presents the mysteries or esoteric meanings of those verses of the Qur'ān that deal with Genesis and the Creation and their purpose, Man and his ultimate destiny. It contains a section on the esoteric meaning of the abbreviated letters at the beginning of certain chapters of the Qur'ān.

3. *Mafātiḥ al-ghayb* (The Keys to the Invisible World).[4] This is his introduction to his commentary on the Qur'ān, in which he discusses the method and principles for the commentary on the Qur'ān, the requisite conditions for the commentary on the Qur'ān and the ethical, metaphysical and spiritual message of the Qur'ān.

---

1. See three articles on the life and doctrines of Mullā Ṣadrā by S. H. Nasr in his *Islamic Life and Thought*, pp. 158–187; 'Mullā Ṣadrā: His Teachings', chapter 36, pp. 643–661 in *History of Islamic Philosophy*, part 1, edited by S. H. Nasr and O. Leaman; 'The Qur'ānic Commentaries of Mullā Ṣadrā', in *Consciousness and Reality*, pp.45–58; B. Kuspinar, 'Perception: A Way to Perfection in Sadra', in *Transcendent Philosophy*, vol. 1:2, pp. 41–62; J. Morris (ed. and trans.), Mulla Ṣadrā, *Wisdom of the Throne*, pp. 3–50; L. Peerwani, 'Qur'ānic Hermeneutics: The Views of Ṣadr al-Dīn Shīrāzī', in *BRISMES Proceedings*, 1991, pp. 468–477; F. Rahman, *The Philosophy of Mullā Ṣadrā*, pp. 1–23.
2. This treatise is published as a part of the collection of *Rasā'il Falsafī* by Ṣadr al-Dīn al-Shīrāzī, edited by J. Āshtiyānī, pp. 75–121.
3. In the Persian translation by M. Khājawī. The translator did not have access to the original Arabic text.
4. Ṣadr al-Dīn al-Shīrāzī. *Mafātiḥ al-ghayb*, edited by M. Khājawī.

4. *Tafsīr al-Qur'ān al-Karīm*,[1] also known as *al-Tafsīr al-kabīr* (The Great Commentary) on the Qur'ān. It consists of the following:

his commentary on *al-Fātiḥah* (The Opening: Chapter One of the Qur'ān) in five parts;
al-Baqarah (The Cow: Chapter 2:1–65);
Āyat al-kursī (The Throne Verse: Chapter 2:255): an introduction, twenty chapters and a conclusion;
Āyat al-nūr (The Light Verse: Chapter 24:35): an introduction, four chapters and a conclusion; *al-Sajdah* (The Prostration: Chapter 32): an introduction, nine parts and a conclusion;
Ya-sīn (Y-S: Chapter 36): eight principles;
al-Wāqi'ah (The Event: Chapter 56): an introduction and the commentary;
al-Ḥadīd (The Iron: Chapter 57): an introduction, twenty-nine parts and a conclusion;
al-Jumu'ah (The Congregation: Chapter 62): an introduction and twelve parts;
al-Ṭāriq (The Morning Star: Chapter 86): an introduction and the commentary in which he states that great secrets hidden in this chapter were revealed to him by God;
al-A'alā (The Most High: Chapter 87): an introduction and seven chapters;
and *al-Zalzāl* (The Earthquake: chapter 99): an introduction and the commentary.

He also quotes many verses of the Qur'ān and comments upon them in his philosophical works. In a sense, the whole of the corpus of Mullā Ṣadrā is related to Qur'ānic commentary, and all of his Qur'ānic commentaries are replete with theological, metaphysical and theosophical discussions and his intellectual intuitions (*mukāshifāt*). They mark the synthesis of four different traditions of the Qur'ānic commentary before him, the Shī'ite, theological, philosophical and Ṣūfī, as well as Ṣadrā's own metaphysical insights.

---

1. *Ibid.*, and *Tafsīr al-Qur'ān al-Karīm*, 7 volumes, edited by M. Khājawī.

In this section I shall be briefly looking at Ṣadr al-Dīn Shirāzī's hermeneutics of the Qur'ān. By hermeneutics I mean a general body of methodological principles that underlie interpretation as well as the epistemological assumptions of understanding.

Ṣadrā's hermeneutics of the Qur'ān yields much interesting material, but here we will briefly look into the following areas: (a) his principles of exegesis (*tafsīr*); (b) the requisite conditions for the hermeneutics of the Qur'ān; (c) existential reading of the Qur'ān; (d) description of some features of Ṣadrā's *Tafsīr*.

Principles that Underlie Ṣadrā's Hermeneutics of the Qur'ān

In general the principles of Ṣadrā's commentary do not differ much from the Shī'ite[1] and Ṣūfī *tafsīr*s of the Qur'ān. But before discussing those principles I shall briefly give the epistemological assumptions behind his exegesis. According to Ṣadrā, there are three interconnected levels of the created world: the physical world, the imaginary world and the world of intellect. Whatever exists in the physical world is an apparition of the imaginary world, which in turn is an apparition of its reality that exists in the knowledge of God.[2]

Man's being has also three basic interconnected levels: (a) the sensory level or the realm of five external senses; (b) the level of imagination, which also has five senses but they are interior senses; (c) the intellectual (spiritual) level. In the intellectual level the realities of things exist without matter and representation, or they are universal, cognitive realities; in the level of imagination things exist with forms but without physical matter; and the physical or sensory level is the concrete or tangible level of Man. Now whatever exists in the intellectual level has its similitude in the imaginary

1. For the principles of Shī'ī *tafsīr* see 'Allāmah Sayyid M. H. Ṭabāṭabā'ī. *The Qur'ān in Islam*, chapter 2, pp. 25–61; M. Ayoub, 'The Speaking Qur'ān and the Silent Qur'ān: A Study of the Principles and Development of Imāmī Shī'ī *tafsīr*', pp. 177–198, in A. Rippin (ed.), *Approaches to the History of the Interpretation of the Qur'ān*.
2. Ṣadr al-Dīn al-Shīrāzī. *Mafātiḥ al-ghayb*, *op. cit.*, p. 95.

level, and whatever exists in the imaginary level has its similitude in the sensory level.

Likewise, the divine revelation also has three basic levels. The highest level is that of the Speech of God, which is simple; it is His attribute and not separate from His essence.[1] Lower than that is the imaginative or revelation the symbolic level of the divine Speech, and the lowest level is the sensory, linguistic level, which is the Book of God. But all these levels are interconnected and correspond with each other. As Ṣadrā states: 'This Qur'ān, which is manifest before us, is both the Speech of God and His Book'; 'they are one in essence, different in expression.'[2] In other words, the divine at its highest level is simple, non-composite and without forms; at the lowest level it is composite, material and in the linguistic form; the intermediate level is symbolic and non-material but has forms. Just as human speech at the highest level is non-composite and cognitive, lower than that is its level of representation in forms and symbols, and at the lowest level, which is the sensory level, it is expressed linguistically. But the speaker and the speech are not separated from each other, nor are the cognitive, imaginative and sensory levels separated from each other. Rather, all are interconnected and correspond with each other. The highest is the cognitive level and the lowest is the sensory level.[3]

On the basis of the above levels of the divine revelation, Ṣadrā explains how Prophet Muḥammad, according to the three basic levels of his being, could have received the divine revelation.[4] He states that the spirit of the Prophet crossed the sensory level of his being and then the level of imagination, and at the separation from matter, from physical time and material dimensions, it ascended to the intellectual level and perceived the Speech of God immediately. Then his spirit descended the way it had ascended to the level of intellect, crossing the imaginary level, and arrived at the sensory level. The divine Speech which he perceived also changed its levels from the cognitive-spiritual to the imaginary and then to the

1. *Ibid.* and *Asfār, op. cit.*, vol. 7, p. 8.
2. *Ibid.*, pp. 22, 10.
3. *Ibid.*, p. 10.
4. *Ibid.*, pp. 24–25.

sensory, corresponding to the three levels of his being. Thus, at reaching the physical, sensory level, the revelation and the spiritual words became transformed into human language and acquired the shape of writing.

Let us come back to some principles we observe in Ṣadrā's hermeneutics of the Qur'ān.

1. The levels or depths of the Qur'ān. The Qur'ān, according to Ṣadrā, is like 'being' or 'existence', which has three basic levels. He bases this theory on his interpretation of the famous verse of the Qur'ān (8:5) concerning the three modes of receiving the divine revelation: 'It is not for a human that God should speak to him [directly] but through inspiration [i.e. at the intellective level, as Ṣadrā would say] or behind a veil [i.e. in symbols, for Ṣadrā] or He may send a messenger who inspires him by God's permission [i.e. at the external, literal level, as Ṣadrā would have it].'[1] In other words, the Scripture according to Ṣadrā has three principal hermeneutic levels: intellective, symbolic and literal. In another place he says: 'Most of the words in the divine Book convey the external, literal meaning, which imply the inner and hidden meaning, which in turn imply another inner and hidden meaning.'[2] In the same context he says in his *Asfār*:[3] 'The Qur'ān, like a man, has inner and outer aspects. Each of them has manifest and hidden meanings. The hidden has another hidden meaning, and so on till the ultimate limit, which is known only to God, for *ta'wīl* [lit. to take a thing back to its origin] of its ultimate meaning is known to God alone' (Qur'ān, 3:7). Then he quotes a tradition attributed to the Prophet: 'The Qur'ān has inner and outer meanings, the inner further has another meaning, and so on to seven other meanings that are encoded in each meaning.'[4] In another place he quotes a tradition of 'Alī ibn Abī Ṭālib, who is reported to have said: 'There is no verse of the Qur'ān that does not possess exoteric (*ẓāhir*), esoteric (*bāṭin*),

1. *Ibid.*, p. 9.
2. *Ibid.*
3. *Ibid.*, p. 36.
4. For the Shī'ite source of this tradition cf. Ṭabāṭabā'ī. *The Qur'ān in Islam*, p. 30.

limit (*ḥadd*) and the primary meaning (*maṭla'*).'[1] Commenting on this tradition he says: 'The exoteric is what is understood (literally) from its words before the mind (reflects) on it, the esoteric is the inherent notions in the first (literal) meanings, the limit is where the perception of human minds and intellects reaches its ultimate end to perceive further (its meanings) and the primary meaning is the divine mysteries and divine indications that are perceived by way of spiritual unveiling and witnessing.'[2] This implies that the Qur'ān has many vertical levels of meanings perceived according to the intellectual and spiritual capacity of the believer, and the being of the Qur'ān constantly invites new interpretation to reveal the infinite potentiality of its meaning. It is dynamic in nature and not static. What we find in Ṣadrā's theory of Scriptural language, which is basically the Shī'ite and Ṣūfī theory, anticipates what P. Ricoeur says in the context of Scriptural language, namely, that it is symbolic in nature. By symbol Ricoeur means any structure of meaning in which a direct, primary, literal sense designates in addition to another sense, which is indirect and secondary and which can be apprehended only through the first. So the hermeneutic task consists in deciphering the hidden meaning in the apparent, in unfolding the levels of meaning implied in the literal apparent meaning.[3]

2. The Qur'ān having exoteric and esoteric levels, leads us to the second principle of Ṣadrā, according to which some verses of the Qur'ān are explicit (*muḥkam*) and some are equivocal (*mutashābih*) in nature. Equivocality, as defined by Izutsu, normally implies uncertainty, indetermination and ambiguousness in the use of a word, and that the word in its basic structure has a number of different meanings. If, for instance, the Arabic word *'ayn'* is used without any clarifying context, it could mean many diverse things such as 'spring', 'eye',

1. *Mafātiḥ, op. cit.*, p. 70; *'Tafsīr Sūrah al-Sajdah'*, in *Tafsīr al-Qur'ān al-Karīm, op. cit.*, vol.. 6, p. 23.
2. *Mafātiḥ*, p. 485.
3. Paul Ricoeur, *The Conflict of Interpretations*, pp. 13–14.

'source', 'essence' or 'prominent leader'. In this kind of polysemy the different meanings are given to the word *'ayn'* and the meanings stand in the same dimension. This is what Izutsu calls 'horizontal polysemy'.[1] Ṣadrā uses this type of polysemy, but according to him it is the first and lowest level of the Qur'ān, or its surface meaning. For Ṣadrā the Qur'ān is polysemic vertically, again to use Izutsu's terminology, that is to say, one word or expression is multi-dimensional in meaning and is used significantly at different levels. For instance, the word 'throne' in the Qur'ānic verse 25:59, according to Ṣadrā, signifies externally the heart of man; its inner meaning or inner throne is his animal spirit, the 'inner' of the inner meaning being his spiritual heart or rational soul, which is the substratum or throne for the establishment of his spirit. This spirit is a higher luminous substance.[2] Here the same word is used at different levels, but the meanings differ, and all these meanings are authentic for Ṣadrā, because they are perceived at different levels of human consciousness. So, what occurs in the change of meanings is that the human consciousness or soul changes from one level to another level of its being and derives a different shade of meaning subtler than before as it ascends vertically within itself, just as in the seven notes of the sol-fa scale, from the first note, 'do', to the seventh, 'ti', the sound acquires a subtler quality as it ascends. This is the crux of Ṣadrā's philosophical psychology, which asserts that man's being has three basic levels: sensory-empirical, imaginative-rational and spiritual- intellectual. He states in the same work that most of the words in the divine Book are universal realities. Sometimes they are perceived to be in the literal sensible sense, sometimes they are perceived to have inner meaning and inner truth and at yet other times they seem to have the inner meaning of the inner meaning or the inner truth of the inner truth. This perception is based on the same principles as of the cosmos and its emergent states, which are basically three: this world, the next world and the divine world.

---

1. Cf. T. Izutu, *Creation and the Timeless Order of Things*, chapter 4, pp. 98–117.
2. Ṣadr al-Dīn al-Shīrāzī, *Mafātiḥ al-ghayb*, *op. cit.*, p. 88.

All these worlds correspond with each other. So anything found in one of these worlds is found in the other two.[1] All human beings do not operate intensively on all these levels. Some are at the sensory level, some at the imaginative, some at both, some at all three levels. Besides, weakness and intensity in these levels for them also varies, so they perceive the world accordingly. This applies to man's perception of the Book of God as well.

Hence Ṣadrā is critical of those who adhere to the commentaries on the Qur'ān given only by Ibn 'Abbās (d. 68/87), Qutādah (d. 118/736), Mujāhid ibn Jabr (d. 104/722), Muqātil ibn Sulaymān (d. 150/767), etc. and disparage the rest of the commentaries on the Qur'ān, especially the Ṣūfī and gnostic commentaries, as 'commentary according to one's opinion' (*tafsīr bi'l-ra'y*). According to Ṣadrā the tradition of the Prophet, which states that 'whoever makes the commentary on the Qur'ān according to his own opinion prepares for himself a place in the Fire',[2] is sound. But it means (a) a person has an opinion about something to which his nature and caprice incline, and he allows his own views to influence the commentary on the Qur'ān; (b) someone interprets the Qur'ān having little knowledge of the Arabic language of the Qur'ān and the science of the Qur'ān, and having no knowledge of the mystical unveilings and insight into the Qur'ān. He quotes 'Alī ibn Abī Ṭālib who is reported to have said: 'If the meaning of the Qur'ān was limited to the external, linguistic meaning, there would not have occurred differences of opinion [among the scholars regarding the meaning of the content of the Qur'ān]. This difference can be removed only if a person is given to the deeper understanding of the meaning of the Qur'ān.'[3]

3. The third principle one notices is the harmony between the intellect (*'aql*) and the divine revelation in Ṣadrā's hermeneutics

---

1. *Ibid.*, pp. 87–88.
2. This tradition is recorded by al-Tirmidhī in his book on *Tafsīr*, which begins with a chapter entitled 'Concerning that which has befallen him who comments on the Qur'ān according to his own opinion'.
3. Ṣadr al-Dīn al-Shīrāzī. *Mafātiḥ al-ghayb*, *op. cit.*, pp. 63, 69–70.

of the Qur'ān. The former, according to him, is the internal proof (*ḥujjah*) of God in man, and the latter is the external proof of God for man. He also calls the intellect the divine law (*shar'*) within man and the divine law (*Shar'*) as the intellect external to man.[1] He defines the role of intellect in connection with the Qur'ān in the following manner: The Qur'ānic revelation is the light that causes one to 'see'. Intellect is the eye that sees and that contemplates this light. In order for the phenomenon of vision to be produced, there must be light, but it is necessary to have eyes to see. If you suppress this light, your eyes will not see anything; if you obstinately close your eyes, as do the literalists and jurists, you will not see anything either. In both cases there is a triumph of darkness. But to complement the divine revelation with the intellect is to have 'light upon light', as the Light Verse of the Qur'ān (24:35) says.[2] Ṣadrā follows this principle in all his works.

The Fourfold Method of Exegesis of the Qur'ān

From the commentaries available to him Ṣadrā observes four different methods of approach to the commentary on the Qur'ān.

a. Methodology adopted by philologists, jurists, traditionists and the followers of Aḥmad ibn Ḥanbal (d. 241/855). Ṣadrā's critique of this methodology is that the commentators adhere to the lexical and literal meaning of the words and verses in the Qur'ān, even if such a meaning defies rational principles. According to him, such an approach to the Qur'ān shows the intellectual weakness and limitation of those who adhere to it. This could be due to 'the dominance of the external laws [of *Sharī'ah*] over them and the deficiency in their understanding to perceive the intention of the Qur'ān and the mysteries of the verses. So, what

1. *'Tafsīr sūrah al-Baqarah'*, in *Tafsīr al-Qur'ān al-Karīm*, vol. 2, p. 31.
2. *Sharḥ Uṣūl al-Kāfī: kitāb al-'aql wa al-jahl*, edited by M. Khājawī, p. 166; also H. Corbin in his *En islam iranien*, vol. 4, p. 74.

overtakes them while listening to the inner meaning (*ta'wīl*) [of the Qur'ān] is like what overtakes the eyes of bats when the [rays] of light fall on them.'[1] He states further: 'The greatest calamity, of which man is unaware [but] keeps him from perceiving the deeper truths of the Qur'ān, is caused by man's arrogant adherence to the literal meaning of the Scripture only.'[2] 'If such a person claims that there is no other meaning of the Qur'ān except what is given in the literal exegesis [of the Qur'ān], then he gives information about the limit of his self, [and he] is right in that. But he has erred in relegating all the people to the level of his understanding that is his habitation, his station, his limit and his foothold. And how can the state of a traveller, rather, of a flier be compared with the state of one who is stationary? Nay, the chronicles and reports indicate that the field of meanings of the Qur'ān is vast for the travelling of the people of understanding, and its space is vast for the flight of the companions of yearning and ecstasy.'[3]

b. Methodology adopted by rationalist philosophers. According to Ṣadrā the rationalist philosophers interpret the Qur'ānic verses and words in ways that are agreeable to their reason and that correspond to their principles of inquiry and reflective premises, which are allegorical and far-fetched in meaning. In doing so, they invalidate the apparent or literal meaning of the Qur'ān.[4]

c. Methodology that is a mixture of the above two methodologies, adopted by most of the Mu'tazilites among them al-Zamakhsharī, (d.538/1144) and *Mutakallimūn* (Kalām theologians). They interpret the verses of the Qur'ān that pertain to the Creation in a rational way and adhere to the apparent or literal meaning of the verses that deal with the Resurrection and Return.

---

1. *Mafātiḥ al-ghayb*, p. 69.
2. '*Tafsīr sūrah al-Sajdah*', in *Tafsīr al-Qur'ān al-Karīm*, *op. cit.*, vol.. 6, pp. 10–11.
3. *Mafātiḥ al-ghayb*, p. 69.
4. '*Tafsīr Āyat al-kursī*', in *Tafsīr al-Qur'ān al-Karīm*, vol. 4, pp. 162; 166.

d. Methodology adopted by those who are 'well-grounded in knowledge', and those whom God chooses for the unveiling of the truths, the spiritual meanings, the divine mysteries and indications in the revelation and the secrets of *ta'wīl* (lit. taking a thing back to its origin, i.e., esoteric meaning), so when they unveil a particular meaning, a divine indication or a truth, they establish that meaning without invalidating its apparent meaning and without destroying the basis of inner meaning, without the meaning's being contrary to the literal meaning, because these are the conditions and signs of unveiling (*mukāshifah*) of the esoteric meaning.[1]

He suggests that one should either adhere to the literal meaning of the Scripture without altering its meaning and giving its interpretation, or be an esoteric gnostic well-grounded in the realization of the truths and the deeper meanings of the Scripture, who holds to the literal meanings as well as the esoteric meanings of the Scripture. One should not be among those who interpret the Qur'ān according to their unbridled wit and oblique insight, giving rational philosophical meanings and common universal notions and giving up the literal meanings of the Scripture, because that amounts to the invalidation of the Sharī'ah.[2] For the inner meanings and mysteries of the Qur'ān, according to him, do not contradict the literal meanings, rather they are additional to it and enrich it. It is like arriving at the essence or kernel from the shell, so the external meanings are the moulds of the inner realities. However, esoteric meaning is derived through the spiritual unveiling and divine self-manifestation occurs according to the measure of one's gnosis and the purity of one's heart.[3]

The last method, according to Ṣadrā, is the only complete method to understand the inner mysteries of the Qur'ān. The spiritual unveilings cannot be learned by the lexical rules of Arabic grammar and philology, for if that were possible, he states, then all

1. *Mafātiḥ al-ghayb*, pp. 73–75; '*Tafsīr Āyat al-kursī*', in *Tafsīr al-Qur'ān al-Karīm*, vol. 4, pp. 162, 166.
2. '*Tafsīr Āyat al-kursī*', in *Tafsīr al-Qur'ān al-Karīm*, vol. 4, p. 168.
3. *Ibid.*, pp. 161–162.

the Arabic scholars would have been able to decipher the whole of the Qur'ān. Nor can one arrive at the inner reality of the Scripture through the rules of logic and rational inquiry alone; otherwise the rationalist philosophers would have arrived at it.[1]

Conditions for the Hermeneutics of the Qur'ān

Ṣadrā gives the following conditions for those who wish to comment upon the Qur'ān:

1. To have a thorough knowledge of Arabic language in order to have sound understanding of the literal meaning of the Qur'ān, for that guarantees a sound understanding of the apparent meaning (*ẓāhir*) of the Qur'ānic language. The outward meaning of the text should be established according to the accepted rules of linguistic and literary usages [of Arabic]. This is a prerequisite for any attempt to arrive at a deeper level of the Scripture.[2]

2. To practise the religious discipline and the ethical code in order to purify the soul and refine its 'mystery' (*sirr*, i.e. inner level of the soul) in order to understand the divine revelation at different levels through spiritual unveilings. This entails: detachment from the possession of riches except for the necessities so that the heart does not get preoccupied with material wealth; detachment from worldly ambitions and aspirations; the resolve not to follow anyone or anything (in religion) without reflection (*taqlīd*); not limiting oneself to purely juridical meaning of the Scripture; repentance for sins committed and determination not to do them again.[3]

3. To have the knowledge of the existing commentaries on the Qur'ān, the science of the Qur'ān and Ḥadīth.

---

1. *'Mutashābihāt al-Qur'ān'*, in *Rasā'il Falsafī*, *op. cit*,. pp. 76–77, 88.
2. *'Tafsīr sūrah al-Ḥadīd'*, in *Tafsīr al-Qur'ān al-Karīm*, vol. 6, p. 141.
3. *Kasr asnām al-jāhilīyya*, edited by M. T. Dāneshpazhuh, p. 133.

4. There should be harmony between the divine revelation and intellect in the exegesis.

5. To be blessed by God to receive deeper mysteries and meanings of the Qur'ān through intellectual intuition or spiritual unveiling (*kashf*), illumination (*ishrāq*), vision (*shuhūd*) or divine self-manifestation, which do not contradict the literal or surface meaning of the Qur'ān. These conditions in general are observed in his hermeneutics of the Qur'ān.

Existential Recitation of the Qur'ān

In order to arrive at a deeper understanding of the divine revelation, Ṣadrā gives the following guidance.[1]

1. Purification of the 'heart' from malicious sins and corrupted beliefs, as God says: 'only the pure ones can touch it' [Qur'ān, 56:79].

2. Presence of the 'heart' [or attentiveness of the mind] and refraining from the inner chattering of the ego (*nafs*) while reciting the Qur'ān. This quality is born when the 'heart' [or mind] is purified from the objectives (*aghrāḍ*) of one's ego. If one is able to remove from his heart the love of something futile then there will grow in his heart the love of reality (*al-ḥaqq*).

3. Reflection on what one is reading (in the Qur'ān). This is other than having the presence of mind. A person may certainly read the Qur'ān without occupying his mind with something else, but may nevertheless limit himself to listening to the recitation of the Qur'ān without reflecting on what he is reciting, whereas the real purpose behind its recitation is the reflection on it, which is also the spirit of all worship. It is reported that the Commander of

---

1. *Mafātiḥ al-ghayb*, pp. 58–69. Some of these conditions are also mentioned by Abū Ḥāmid al-Ghazzālī in his *Iḥyā' al-'ulūm al-Dīn*, vol. 1, pp. 248 ff.

the Faithful ('Alī ibn Abī Ṭālib) said: 'There is no good in any worship if there is no understanding (*fiqh*) of the intention behind it, and no good in the recitation of the Qur'ān without reflection on it.' It is reported about the Prophet that once when he recited the Qur'ānic verse 'In the name of God the Merciful, the Compassionate' he repeated it twenty times in order to reflect on it. And when the verse [3:190] 'In the changing of day to night there are signs for those who reflect' was revealed, he said: 'Woe to him who recites the Qur'ān but does not reflect upon it.'

4. Inference (*istinbāṭ*). This is the seeking from every divine verse of the understanding that is appropriate to it, for there is not a single domain of knowledge whose principle and derivation, origin and end are not given in the Qur'ān. The highest science of the Qur'ān constitutes the knowledge of divine Names, His Attributes, His Acts and the knowledge of the next world. As for the divine Acts, they are (His creation of) the heavens and the earth and what is in them. A reflective person (*mudabbir*) perceives the truths behind them, that is, their natures, which is the science of Nature and the science of creation; their modes, positions, beautiful order and organization, which is the science of Mathematics and of Allotment (*qadar*); their principles and goals, which is the science of non-material beings, the science of Decree (*qaḍā'*)[1] and the celestial kingdom. The reflection on the divine Acts leads one to the divine Attributes and Names, and this is the knowledge of divine Unity. For the Act indicates the Agent and His greatness. One who knows from the Act only the motion and measure knows only the Agent as Mover and Giver of forms. But contemplation on the divine Act, that is, penetrating the mysteries of the divine Acts, leads one to witness in the divine Act not just His Act but the Agent himself, and he who knows the reality sees Him in everything and everywhere. For everything is from Him, is returning to Him and is by Him

1. By 'Decree' Ṣadrā means the universal forms of all things in the world of intellect, and by 'Allotment' he means the particular forms of all things in the world of soul. Cf. his '*Tafsīr sūrah al-Ḥadīd*', in *Tafsīr al-Qur'ān al-Karīm*, vol. 6, pp. 252–253, etc.

and for Him. He is the totality in His unity according to the spiritual investigation. Whoever does not see Him in all has not seen Him. It is reported that the Commander of the Faithful ('Alī ibn Abī Ṭālib) said: 'I do not see anything but God in it; he who knows Him knows that anything devoid of Him is futile and everything is evanescent except His Face.' That is to say, everything is evanescent if considered as something that exists by itself and not as something that exists thanks to God and His power. This is one of the keys to the knowledge of spiritual unveiling (*kashf*).

5. Removal of the obstacles to understanding (the meaning of the Qur'ān). This is other than purifying the mind from the filthy sins and wicked, blameworthy qualities. There are many obstacles to the understanding of the meanings of the Qur'ān, other than those aforementioned. The mind for the perception of truths of things is like a mirror reflecting the forms that are the objects of sight. Just as some of the veils of mirror are internal, such as its (lowly) nature (or low quality of the mirror), rust or its unpolished surface, and some are external, such as the existence of an obstacle (in front of it) or the placing of the mirror at such an angle that the object intended to be seen in it is out of focus, so too some of the veils of the mind that prevent the understanding (of the meanings of the Qur'ān) are internal and some are external. The internal veils may derive from privation and imperfection, such as child-mindedness, feeble-mindedness and simple ignorance (i.e. lacking knowledge), or they may be existential, such as sins and vices. He who persists in sinning or has the attributes of pride and jealousy will never have the greatness of the reality disclosed (*tajallī*) to him, because his mind has become unclear and rusty. For whenever the appetites gather intensity, the meanings of the Qur'ān become heavily veiled. Thus the heart (or mind) is like a mirror, the lower appetites are like rust and the meanings of the Qur'ān are like forms that are seen in it. The discipline for the mind in order to subjugate the appetites is like polish applied to the mirror to

improve its clarity. As for the external veils, some pertain to privation, such as the absence of reflection (on what one is reciting in the Qur'ān). Reflection is the movement of the mind from the principles to the conclusions. The absence of reflection is like a mirror angled such that its surface does not clearly reflect the object that is the intended to be seen in it.

Some veils are existential in nature, such as common beliefs based on blind conformity or ignorance of metaphysical matters. These are like a cover for the mirror or an opaque obstacle like a wall or mountain before it. They are of four kinds:

a. Spending one's entire energy (*al-himmah*) on the philology, grammar and syntax (of the language of the Qur'ān).

b. Blindly following the religious doctrine heard from the masters (*shuyūkh*) and holding to it adamantly, and becoming fanatic in following only that which one has heard, without reflection and insight into that doctrine. Such a person, whose belief has limited him, has halted at what he has heard, so it is impossible for him to transcend his station. There is a Ṣūfī saying: 'Knowledge is a veil (to the perception of the reality of the things as they are).' By 'knowledge' is meant the beliefs to which the majority cling blindly or adherence to the (religious) disputations conveyed by the fanatics of some religious doctrines. Knowledge that is attained through intellectual intuition (or unveiling) and vision by the light of spiritual insight, however, is never a veil. How could it be, because it is the very purpose and goal of the object of desire?

c. Engrossment in the knowledge (of the Qur'ān) and going into the minutest details about the grammar and syntax (of the text of the Qur'ān), thereby spending one's entire life in such research. The basic purpose of the revelation of the Qur'ān is to drive people to the vicinity of God by the perfection of their essences and illumination of their hearts (or minds) by the light of the knowledge of God and His signs. It is not to spend one's time finding the (grammatical) beauty of the divine Word, the science of rhetoric, the science of figure of speech and eloquence (in the Qur'ān). These are secondary matters used for arguing with those who deny (the Qur'ān as the Word of God).

d. The fourth veil is remaining firm and adhering to commentaries on the Qur'ān given by Ibn 'Abbās, Qutādah, Mujāhid, Muqātil, etc., and considering any other commentary besides those as 'commentary according to one's own opinion' (*tafsīr bi'l-ra'i*).

6. He who recites the Qur'ān should perceive that the Qur'ān is addressed to him particularly, for the Qur'ān could repeatedly reveal itself to the inner self of man. The descent and manifestation of the Qur'ān are according to the state of one's heart and level of existence. The Prophet is reported to have said of those who only memorize the words of the Qur'ān without deep reflection on them: 'They recite the Qur'ān but it does not transcend their throats', in other words, it stays on their tongues and does not reach their hearts.

7. A person should be affected by the recitation and deep reflection on the divine Word, and his states may change according to the different types of messages in the Qur'ān.

8. He should ascend to a level in the recitation at which he hears the divine Word from God and not from himself. There are three levels of the recitation of the Qur'ān. (a) The lowest is the person reciting the Qur'ān before God Who is seeing him and listening to him. This person should be in a state of humility and supplication. (b) He witnesses in his heart as if His Lord is addressing him, showering His grace upon him. His state should be that of humility, veneration, attention and understanding. (c) In the divine Word he sees the Speaker, and his total energy (*himmah*) and attention are directed towards the Speaker. It is as

if he is immersed in the vision of the Speaker and oblivious to everything else. About this level Ja'far al-Ṣādiq [the sixth Shī'ite Imam, d. 148/765], is reported to have said: 'By God! God self-manifests to His creation in the Word (i.e. the Qur'ān), but many have no insight for that.'

The principles and the existential recitation of the divine Message in the Qur'ān given by Ṣadrā are some of the basic tools and steps necessary for the understanding of the divine revelation at multiple levels. They could apply to all the revealed divine Books.

Salient Features of Ṣadrā's Tafsīr

I shall briefly narrate some features of Ṣadrā's hermeneutics of the Qur'ān, which are also found in his exegesis on the Light Verse.

Ṣadrā usually begins his commentary by philological treatment of the verse in question. He often gives a list of divergent opinions on a word or phrase of the Qur'ān emanating from grammarians, and leaves them as they are, even citing contradictory opinions. At times he goes beyond that and tries either to reach some kind of harmonization of the variant opinions or to show that one of the opinions could be given more credence than the others on the basis of certain rules of Arabic grammar. He often cites variant readings (*qirā'ah*) of the Scripture, mostly of the reciters belonging to Kufian and Basran circles, such as Nakha'ī (d. 94/712), Qutādah (d. 118/736), al-Ḥasan al-Baṣrī (d. 110/728) or al-Kisā'ī (d. between 179/795 and 192/807), etc.; he narrates the occasion of revelation (*asbābb al-nuzūl*), that is, the incidents or circumstances with reference to which the revelation came to the Prophet and its surface and esoteric meaning; he elaborates the obscure and difficult words of the Qur'ān (*gharā'ib al-Qur'ān*) and also gives their interpretation according to his insight, mystical experience and epistemology; he interprets the Qur'ān by the Qur'ān. Another distinctive feature of his *Tafsīr* is that he records the interpretation of the verse or word in question given by theologians, philosophers, the Qur'ān exegetes, etc.; he either accepts their interpretation or critiques it and gives his own interpretation. The Qur'ān exegetes he quotes for the most part are the Mu'tazilite exegete al-Zamakhsharī (d. 538/1144), the Shī'ite commentators al-Qummī (d. 328/939) and al-Ṯabarasī (d. 548/1153) and the Ash'arite theologian-commentator Fakhr al-Dīn al-Rāzī (d. 606/1209); he records the interpretation of the Prophet and the Shī'ite Imams, Ṣūfīs and gnostics (*'urafā'*) and further gives its deeper meaning.

What strikes a reader most in his *Tafsīr* is his philosophical meditation on the Qur'ān, and also his statements now and then that this or that meaning of the divine verse was unveiled to him by intellectual inspiration from the divine Throne, or there was divine epiphany or divine illumination of it. Hence he states time and again that, 'nothing of that which the exoteric commentators on the Qur'ān, such as al-Zamakhsharī and those who emulate him, have written is the true knowledge of the Qur'ān, or the gnosis of the divine revelation in the true sense. All of that relates to philology, grammar and dialectic, and touches only the shell of the exterior revetment. The true knowledge of the Qur'ān is something else.'[1] That something else for Ṣadrā is the knowledge that pertains to the metaphysical realm, the knowledge of God and His creation and man's soul through spiritual unveiling. This is very obvious when one reads his vast commentary. But besides his mystical insights and rational demonstration of his receiving those insights from the surface meaning of the divine revelation, he also plays the role of a spiritual guide to the divine Realm. He gives numerous discourses with demonstrations about the spiritual path, its ethics and discipline on the basis of the Qur'ān, the Ḥadīth of the Prophet complemented by the teaching of the Shī'ite Imams, sages, gnostics, Ṣūfīs and ancient philosophers such as Socrates, Plato and Plotinus, etc.

1. Ṣadr al-Dīn al-Shīrāzī, *Se Aṣl*, edited by S. H. Nasr, p. 84.

Conclusion

In analysing the views of Ṣadrā regarding the nature of the Qur'ān, its levels of meanings and methods of commentary, we are informed of an approach that may be counted among one of the most spiritualistic and gnostic orientations that appeared in the Islamic world. It indicates a narrative of the history of the soul and its potential, and a guide towards a full-fledged spiritual life.

The content of his *Tafsīr* is philosophical and mystical-gnostic in nature based on his transcendent theosophy. If one were to characterize the central issues that arise from the commentary, they seem moral, philosophical, esoteric and gnostic in nature. Insofar as morality may be seen to have relationship to law, and the law to the state, an argument could perhaps be mounted to claim a specifically political significance for all the passages that he has treated as moral issues. Implicitly such themes do convey the message that if every individual takes the responsibility of morally and spiritually reforming himself according to the way he has indicated to study and reflect on the message of the Scripture and act upon it, then the whole of society could become reformed. Explicitly, however, he seldom deals with the nature of a polity or the conduct of state.

The *Tafsīr* of this genre, according to our research, is unique in the Islamic religious literature. It has had a great impact on the subsequent commentaries on the Qur'ān including the most recent one, *al-Mīzān* of Allāmah Ṭabāṭabā'ī (d. 1982).

Summary of the Text

The hermeneutics of the Light Verse was completed by Mullā Ṣadrā in 1030/1620. In this work he synthesizes the long tradition of commentaries upon this verse .The present translation is based on volume four of the *Tafsīr al-Qur'ān al-Karīm* by Ṣadr al-Dīn al-Shīrāzī, critically edited by M. Khājawī (Qum: Bīdār, 1403/1982), which also contains Ṣadrā's exegesis on *Āyāt al-kursī* (the Throne

Verse). The exegesis of the Light Verse runs to eighty-seven pages from 343 to 427 of this volume, which are mentioned in the square brackets of this translation. It contains an introduction and four chapters. The introduction identifies the purpose of the work. The first chapter is the exegesis of 'God is the Light of the heavens and the earth; the similitude of His Light is as a niche'. In this chapter he gives the possible meanings of the term 'light' that were proposed by Muslim thinkers before him, especially the Peripatetic philosophers, Illuminationist philosophers and Ṣūfis, including Abū Ḥāmid al-Ghazzālī whose definition of light, according to him, was compatible with the understanding of the 'Imams of wisdom'. But Ṣadrā goes deeper than al-Ghazzālī in his interpretation of 'light', which, according to him, is not only something that makes things visible as al-Ghazzālī had defined but is also 'a perfection of existence'. Existence and Light are identical in meaning and reality, but different in name.

In chapter two he continues with the exegesis of 'the similitude of His Light is as a niche wherein is a lamp; the lamp is in a glass; the glass is like a glittering star'. He gives several interpretations of 'niche', 'lamp' and 'glass', some derived from Ṣūfī sources, and further gives several interpretations according to his ontology. For instance, he interprets 'lamp' as a similitude of existence, and 'niche' as quiddity; or 'lamp' as a similitude of the divine Light and 'glass' as the Prophet Muḥammad, or 'light' as a similitude of the divine Essence and 'lamp' as the divine Name 'Allah'.

In chapter three he continues with the exegesis of the next part of the Light Verse, 'kindled from a blessed tree, an olive that is neither of the Orient nor of the Occident'. He gives various interpretations of the 'olive tree' and the 'olive oil', and gives two other interpretations of the Light Verse, one pertaining to microcosm, namely the physical human body, and the other given by Avicenna, which pertains to the four levels of the rational soul.

In chapter four he concludes the exegesis of the remainder of the Light Verse 'God guides to His Light whom He wills'. He interprets God's Light as '*nūr Muḥammadī*' (Muḥammadan light) which according to him is identical with the First Intellect, and the divine

Name 'Allah', which is inclusive of the rest of the divine Names. This long chapter deals with the self-disclosure of the divine Light in the Perfect Man, his qualities, his role as a vicegerent of God on the earth and a teacher of mankind on metaphysical matters.

In his conclusion and testament Ṣadrā cautions readers not to divulge the treasures of realities, symbols, illuminations and divine self-disclosures revealed to him, which he had written in this text to those who reject gnosis and shun metaphysical matters because they are the enemies of wisdom and lovers of caprice. He gives guidance to wayfarers on the path of mystical gnosis about the discipline required for reaching the ultimate goal of the soul, which is none but the Absolute Existence or the divine Light.

Studies on the Light Verse of Ṣadrā

Besides some articles by Seyyed Hossein Nasr on Ṣadrā's[1] commentaries on the Qur'ān in general, there is one doctoral thesis by Muḥsin Ṣāliḥ presented to the Temple University in 1993. The author has translated and analysed *Tafsīr Āyat al-Nūr* by Ṣadrā. But I have not had access to this work. I myself have written on essay on this work,[2] in which I have surveyed in general Ṣadrā's methodology of exegesis in his *Tafsīr al-Kabīr* and in particular in his exegesis of the Light Verse.

1. S. H. Nasr. 'Qur'ānic Commentaries of Mullā Ṣadrā', in *Consciousness and Reality: Studies in Memory of Toshihiko Izutsu*, edited by S. J. Āshtiyānī and others, pp. 45–47; also *Ṣadr al-Dīn Shīrāzī and His Transcendent Theosophy*, chapter 7, pp. 123–135; and 'Mullā Ṣadrā: His Teachings', in *History of Islamic Philosophy*, part 1, chapter 36, pp. 656–657.
2. L. Peerwani, 'Qur'ānic Hermeneutics: The Views of Ṣadr al-Dīn Shīrāzī', in *BRISMES Proceedings*, 1991, pp. 468–477.

Tafsīr Āyāt al-Nūr
The Hermeneutics of the Light Verse

In the name of God the Most Merciful the Most Compassionate (*Bismillāhir-Raḥmānir-Raḥīm*)

[345] Praise be to God the giver of intelligence, goodness and munificence. Benediction and peace be upon Muḥammad the master of His friends, the axis of the cycle of existence, the point of subtle divine mystery in all beings, the first one intended, the last one to be sent. He was grateful (to God), and God blesses him who is thankful; he is the one through whom the Book (*dīwān*) of divine Message was sealed and the edifice of prophethood completed; by his existence the principles of glory and rules of spiritual chivalry (*al-futūwwah*) were constructed. Most excellent peace and most perfect benedictions be upon his pure progeny, the 'people of the house' (*ahl al-bayt*) liberated from human impurities, enveloped by the sap of divine knowledge.

Now to begin: So says Muḥammad known as Ṣadr al-Dīn ibn Ibrāhim, the seeker of refuge in the threshold of His Lord. These points are in connection with the exegesis of the Light Verse (*āyāt al-nūr*) which has made the people of time (or my contemporaries) smile owing to the originality of its words, and opened the breast of mankind [with happiness] by its beautiful order. With its explication it gives the right guidance and clarifies the truth. An investigator may spend his life in acquiring the tablets of His lights in it and hunting for His elusive mysteries, and it is quite likely that he may get insight [in it] that another person may not. Because every seeking soul gets a portion, big or small, from the light of God, and every broken heart has a share from the mystery of God whether manifest or hidden. So, with the mind through which thoughts of afflictions pass [346] and the face on which the trace of calamities has been etched, I praise my Lord and censure the Time, and am patient in affliction and grief and in the separation from my loved ones and brothers [in faith].

I had been sympathetic to my sight for my tears
But today every mighty one after his departure is insignificant.

I worked and strove hard, and endeavoured to obtain this desire in which [for its fulfilment] I am now engaged with least advantage and means and struggling with time, which wears and enfeebles. I have a heart which the vicissitude of time has furnished, the affairs [of the world] have disturbed, the affliction of discomfort has touched and intense calamity has covered.

O time, although you bring misfortune to the noble people,
If there is anything [of eminence] left, bring it to me.

I begin [this exegesis] by asking God for good success, for indeed in His hand lies the real victory.

[The First] Chapter

[347] His saying, may His name be glorified:

> God is the Light of the heavens and the earth; the similitude of His Light is that of a lamp in a niche.
> (*Allāhu nūrus-samāwāti wa'l-arḍ. Mathalu nūrihi ka-mishkātin*)

The verification of this verse requires an introduction, which is as follows: the word 'light' is not, as those experts on language and Kalām theologians (*aṣḥāb al-kalām*) who are veiled understand it, a subject of the accident (*al-'araḍ*) that subsists by the behaviour of bodies. They have defined it as something that 'does not remain for two moments' and is among one of the imperfect temporal events in existence.[1] Rather, this 'light' is one of the Names of God the Exalted. He is the One who is the illuminator (*munawwir*) of the lights, who actualizes the realities, manifests the ipseities (*al-huwiyyāt*) and existentiates the quiddities (*al-māhiyyāt*).

'Light', in its unqualified sense, bears many meanings according to the multitude; some meanings are equivocal (*bi'l-ishtirāk*), some literal and some metaphorical, such as the light of the sun, the light of the moon, the light of the lamp, the light of intellect, the light of

1. H. A. Wolfson,.in his *The Philosophy of the Kalam*, pp.522ff, gives the views of several dialectical theologians on this matter.

faith, the light of piety (*taqwā*), the light of a ruby, the light of gold, the light of turquoise.

According to the Illuminationist philosophers (*al-Ishrāqiyyūn*) and their followers, such as the Shaykh al-Maqtūl Shihāb al-Dīn [Suhrawardī],[1] to him who unveils their symbols, extracts their treasures, records their sciences, sheds light on their concepts, [348] exposes their stations and explains their allusions, [light] is a simple (*basīṭah*) and self-manifesting reality which brings other things to manifestation.[2] Accordingly, [this reality] can have neither genus (*jins*) nor differentia (*faṣl*) because it is not composed of parts. So it could not have a known definition, nor could it have an unveiling description as it is not hidden from itself. Rather, it is the most manifest of things. It is the opposite of darkness (*al-ẓulmah*) and hiddenness (*al-khafā'*), [just as] negation is opposite of affirmation. So there is no demonstration for it, rather it is the demonstration for everything. Hiddenness and veiling (*al-ḥijāb*) occur to it only by degrees, such as [in the case of] the degree of self-subsisting light (*al-nūr al-qayyūmī*), because of its extreme manifestation (*al-ẓuhūr*) and apparentness. For [what is] intensely manifest and theophanized [or self-disclosed (*tajallā*)] may cause what is manifested to become hidden owing to the abundance of [light] and extreme deficiency of the thing that it illuminates [to receive it], just as one may observe in bats when strong visible sunlight shines in their pupils. If the situation is thus with regard to sensible light, what do you think about the light of intellect, which reaches the peak of intensity and power?

---

1. Suhrawardī al-Maqtūl, Shihāb al-Dīn, Yahya (d. 587/1191) was the founder of the Illuminationist school of philosophy. He took inspiration from both Zoroastrian philosophy and Sufism to modify the dominant Peripatetic school of philosophy. He is the author of several works both in Arabic and Persian. His most famous work is *Ḥikmat al-Ishrāq* (The Philosophy of Illumination).
2. This is the doctrine of the Illuminationist philosophy whose founder was Shihāb al-Suhrawardī (d. 587/1191). Cf. his *Ḥikmat al-Ishrāq*, translated by J. Walbridge and H. Ziai as *The Philosophy of Illumination*, p 113. Also see H. Ziai, *Knowledge and Illumination*, pp. 162–166.

So 'light' is interpreted by some great Ṣūfīs according to the above meaning, as can be derived from their works and symbolic tales (*marmūzāt*). However, there is a difference between their school of thought and that of the Illuminationist philosophers. According to those great [philosophers], although it is a simple reality its essence is subject to variant degrees in intensity and weakness, plurality and multiplicity, and its modes and individualities to differences in necessity and contingency, substantiality and accidentality, self-sufficiency and dependency.

As for the opinion of those 'Peaks' among the noble ones [i.e. the Ṣufīs], these properties do not occur to [the light] with respect to the definition of its essence, but rather with respect to its theophanies (*tajalliyyāt*), determinations (*ta'ayyunāt*), traits and considerations. Thus the reality (*al-ḥaqq*) is one but multiplicity occurs only with respect to its different loci of manifestation (*al-maẓāhir*), mirrors and recipients (*al-qawābil*).[1] It is not unlikely that the difference between the two schools of thought is attributable to their disparity in technical terms and ways of alluding to things, their artistry in clarification and intimation and their ways of summarizing and detailing, but despite that [349] there is agreement among them as far as the foundations and principles are concerned.

What Shaykh Muḥammad al-Ghazzālī[2] mentions in the *Mishkāt al-anwār* [The Niche of the Lights] when he says 'Light is an expression by which things are made visible'[3] is in accord with the statement of the Imams of wisdom.

1. The indication is to the doctrine of the gnostic school of the Spanish Ṣūfī Ibn 'Arabī (d. 638/1240), cf. W. C. Chittick, *The Sufi Path of Knowledge*, pp. 91–92.
2. Abū Ḥāmid al-Ghazzālī (d. 505/1111) was one of the most famous Muslim thinkers, a theologian, jurist and Ṣūfī of the early period of Islam. His most famous works are *Iḥyā' 'ulūm al-Dīn* (The Revivification of the Sciences of Religion), in which he brings out the esoteric meaning of the Islamic practices and ethical ideals, and *Mishkāt al-Anwār*, which is his commentary on the Light Verse of the Qur'ān and a tradition of Prophet Muḥammad.
3. Cf. Al-Ghazzālī, Abū Ḥāmid, *Al-Mishkāt al-Anwār*, translated by D. Buchman as *The Niche of Lights*, p. 23.

*Detailed Reminder (*Tadhkirah Tafṣīliyya*)*

There are many aspects of meanings in His saying 'God is the Light of the heavens and the earth.'

The first aspect is what the majority of Muslim exegetes (of the Qur'ān) and scholars of Arabic cite, relying upon its recitation by the Commander of the Faithful (*Amīr al-Mu'minīn*) ['Alī ibn Abī-Ṭālib], peace be upon him. It is reported that he recited it in the past tense, namely, 'God was the Light of the heavens and the earth.' That means, '[God was] the possessor of the Light of heavens, and the creator (*ṣāḥib*) of the light of heavens' non-metaphorically, or 'The reality was the Light of the twain' metaphorically.

[Al-Zamakhsharī], the author of *al-Kashshāf* says: 'In its apparentness and clarity He likened it to light in accordance with His saying "God is the Friend (*walī*) of believers; He brings them forth from the darkness to the light" [2:257], i.e. "from the falsehood to the truth".' He relates 'light' to the heavens and the earth in one of two meanings: either it denotes the vastness of His illumination (*ishrāq*) and the pervasion of His luminescence so that the heavens and the earth become luminescent for Him, or He intends that the inhabitants of the heavens and the earth derive luminescence by it."[1] Here ends his comment.

Accordingly, the meaning of its recitation in the past tense would be: Indeed God has unfolded the truth and spread it in the heavens and the earth, or He has illuminated the 'hearts' of their inhabitants by the Light of the Reality (*nūr al-ḥaqq*).

In which case the intention behind 'the similitude of His Light' would be the Attribute of the Reality, marvellous in nature, which God has spread in the world, and guides by it the creation towards the way of the good. The similitudes (*al-tashbihāt*) of 'niche', 'lamp',

---

1. *Al-Kashshāf* of Al-Zamakhsharī (the Mu'tazilite commentator on the Qur'ān, d. 538/1148), vol. 3, p. 67.

'glass', 'oil', which occur (in this verse), are all for affirming the manifestation of the Attribute of the Reality (or the Absolute) and its apparentness. As could be said, the reality by which people are guided is like the light in the niche that kindles its lamp by the clean oil; it is in the candlestick of the glass, very transparent in fineness; [350] in its fineness and radiance it resembles one of the most beautiful glittering stars such as Jupiter or Venus. The glass is in a small hollow aperture in the wall which is closed so that the light of the lamp does not spread, but nevertheless the light is very luminescent and very manifest, as is the reality that penetrates the world and is spread out in the creations.

Without doubt, by 'light' in this respect is intended the Qur'ān, because the reality clarifies it, that is, God guides the people by His firm Word (*kalām*), which is a clear truth. God named it 'light' when He said: 'We have sent down to you a clear light' [4:174]. That is because the Qur'ān is the locus of manifestation (*maẓhar*) of the Light of the reality and of divine knowledge (*al-'irfān*), and the illuminator of the hearts of believers. So the reality is the Light and the Qur'ān is its symbol (*mathal*). He gave it the likeness of the 'lamp'. Hence, the 'lamp' is the Word of God; the 'glass' is the heart of gnostic with the lights of its meanings; the 'niche' is his breast; its 'oil' is the assistance of divine emanation (*al-fayḍ al-ilāhī*) obtained from the blessed tree of prophecy and the sacred mode of existence of the chosen one [i.e. the Prophet]. Owing to its perfect balance and the unification of two modes of existence and its disengagement (*tajarrud*) from the two worlds[1] it is neither particular to the Orient, 'the world of spirits' (*'ālam al-arwāḥ*), nor to the Occident, the 'world of apparitions' (or shadows, *'ālam al-ashbāh*). Rather it is the unifier (*jāmi'*) of both ends and yet elevated from both horizons. Its assistance and illumination for hearts would give them light and perfect them before they deduce the knowledge from the Scripture by their meticulous rational faculties, and derive the lights of sciences from the niche of the breasts of scholars and the people of remembrance. With the extremely wide spread of the emanation of

1. That is, the physical world of matter and the psychic world of forms.

the reality and the intensity of its illumination for the hearts of wayfarers (*al-sālikūn*) and ecstatics (*al-majdhubūn*), it illuminates their hearts and makes their spirits luminescent although no fire of human teaching nor fire of the oil kindled from the hammer of pure nature and the fire-steel of cogitation (*al-fikr*) have touched it.

The second aspect is in accordance with the way of the ancient Ṣūfīs and the Imams engaged in the spiritual journey and the purification [of heart]. It is an understanding [derived] from the meaning of the noble verse (of the Qur'ān), for which they have relied upon the recitation of 'Abd'allāh ibn Mas'ūd. Also al-Wāḥidī mentions a narration about him in *al-Wasīt* that [when] he recited 'God is the Light of the heavens and the earth' [351] [he understood] 'the similitude of His Light' to be in the heart (*qalb*) of the believer.

According to this aspect the intention behind the aforementioned 'light' would be what is reported from the Prophet, peace be upon him and upon his progeny, that, when the verse 'Is he whose breast God has opened for the surrender (*al-islām*) so that he follows a light from his Lord [no better than one hard-hearted ...]?' [39:22] descended upon him [or was revealed to him], he was asked [by Muslims]: 'What is the meaning of this light?' He, peace be upon him and upon his progeny, answered: 'It is that light which when kindled in the heart of the believer his breast becomes "wide2 and happy (*insharaḥa*)'. He was asked: 'Is there any sign for it?' He answered: 'Yes, [the human soul] distances itself from the abode of delusion, turning towards the eternal abode, and is prepared for death before its descent."[1]

According to this [narrative] God has given the similitude of 'lamp' for the light of the heart of the believer, because lamp is obtained and ignited by another light, likewise this light is kindled in his

1. Cf. *Aḥādīth-i Mathnawī* by Furūzānfar, no. 412. There seems to be some textual error in this tradition, which has been corrected by collating with the tradition in the above collection. In this collection Furūzānfar has also given several sources of the traditions of the Prophet, which include the six Sunni collections of the *Ḥadīth*.

heart, which is obtained and ignited from the absolute divine Light and self-subsisting Existence. The heart stands for the 'niche'; the spiritual states (*al-aḥwāl*) and spiritual stations (*al-maqāmāt*) awakened in it by the inspiration (*al-ilhām*) of God, which are for the actualization and assistance for this light, stand for the 'oil'; the acts and many transactions full of blessings correspond to the 'blessed tree'. It is obtained at the centre of the orient of the heart and the occident of the corporeal body without being particular to any of the twain; it is neither related to the heart, as are the pure intellectual sciences (*al-ʿulūm al-ʿaqlīyya*), nor to the corporeal body such as the acts of concupiscence (*al-shahwah*) and irascibility (*al-ghaḍab*). Therefore, it can neither be oriental nor occidental. The psychic spirit (*al-rūḥ al-nafsānī*) stands for the 'glass'.

So the order [of interpretation] would be as follows: The lamp is the similitude of the light of guidance of God in the heart of the believer, which is placed in the glass of his psychic spirit, which is placed in the niche of his heart. The lamp is kindled from the oil of the [spiritual] states and stations, which are as if kindled from the inner being (*bāṭin wujūd*) of the spiritual wayfarer although the fire of (divine) epiphany has not touched it. It is awakened (*inbiʿāth*) from the blessed tree of the righteous acts; this latter light, which is the result of the righteous acts and the inheritance of pure transactions (*al-muʿāmilāt*), is twice as powerful as the first light, which is the light of [divine] guidance occurring at the beginning inviting [him] to [352] servitude and obedience [to God's guidance]. When the light at the end joins the light at the beginning, it becomes 'light upon light'.

The third aspect, which Ṣūfīs of recent times have mentioned, is in accordance with the 'possessors of unveilings' (*aṣḥāb al-mukāshifāt*), the 'possessors of immediate tastes' (*arbāb al-adhwāq*) and the 'people of illuminations'.[1] It is based on the doctrines of the

1. Whatever these Ṣūfī terms mean in the Illuminationist philosophy, such as 'spiritual unveilings' (*al-mukāshifāt*), 'spiritual tastes' (*al-adhwāq*), and 'illuminations' (*al-ishrāqāt*), they imply the immediate experience of a certain level (continued...)

Illuminationist philosophers and the ancient sages of Persia, which correspond to the tradition of the Prophet, peace be upon him and upon his progeny. It is a narrative regarding his nocturnal ascent (*mi'rāj*). He was asked about [what the divine] vision (*al-ru'yā'*) was, to which he answered: 'It was a light that I saw', i.e. the Exalted is the Light. Since it is impossible to connect the vision to Him the Exalted, he assigned 'light' to Him the Exalted.

We have already alluded to the investigation into their [i.e. the Illuminationist philosophers'] school of thought regarding light. This is the clarification. When this word is applied to sensible light (*al-nūr al-maḥsūs*) it (means) it is manifest by itself and makes something else manifest.[1] Its property is that it is sensible by the sense of sight, and it makes the objects of sight manifest. There is no problem in applying the word 'light' to it because sensible light itself has no meaning or notion that pertains to this word; rather it is one of the subjects of this word. For if one finds another thing in the world that has this property, this word would equally apply to it. It is comparable to what is said of the meaning of 'scale', namely, that it is 'something by which a thing is weighed' regardless of whether it has a pole and two scales or not, although in this world it is mostly used in the sense of something that has a pole and two scales.

According to this [interpretation] the application of 'light' to Him the Exalted would be based on the notion that it is the corroboration of its meaning and the subject of its name because His essence is absolutely manifest by itself, making others manifest. That is why the Illuminationist philosophers technically apply the [the term] 'Light of the lights' to Him the Exalted.

The 'light', despite being something essential, is not other than the necessary immaterial essences of light, which are the intellects and

---

(...continued)
of reality in the being of the wayfarer.

1. Cf. *supra*, note 42.

souls, except that it is different in perfection and imperfection and in the degrees of intensity and weakness. [353] Therefore, its application to the essences of light is by way of analogical gradation (*al-tashkīk*), because demonstrative proof (*burhān*) cannot be given for essence, but only for its degrees by analogical gradation; this is the case also with the reality of light. It has different degrees of strength and weakness, of perfection and imperfection; its ultimate perfection is the divine Light (*al-nūr al-ilāhī*), which is the self-sufficient (*al-ghanī*) Light; then follow the superior lights divided into the lights of intellects and the lights of souls; then the lower lights divided into the lights of stars and the lights of elements.

In truth, the reality of 'light' and 'existence' (*al-wujūd*) is the same thing. The existence of every thing is its manifestation, accordingly the existence of corporeal bodies (*al-ajsām*) would also be the degrees of Light. However, the Illuminationist philosophers have held that corporeal bodies are not manifest by themselves but through accidental sensible light (*al-nūr al-maḥsūs al-'āriḍ*).[1] Perhaps there is a mystery here, in that what are existent from the corporeal bodies are the properties of their specific forms (*ṣuwar al-naw'īyya*) and their souls and modes (*hay'āt*), which are from the aspect of existence and luminosity and not from their matters and quantities, which are like extended shadows (*ẓalāl mamdūdah*) having no existence. Reflect on this matter. Some more explanation about it follows. The investigation of these discourses needs a wider capacity [to apprehend], and only those who are proficient in two wisdoms [i.e. theoretical and practical] and whom God inspires in this matter will know them.

So according to these definitions the meaning of His saying 'God is the Light of the heavens and earth' would correspond to the meaning of their saying '[God is] the Light of lights' (*nūr al-anwār*) or the 'Existence of existences' (*wujūd al-wujūdāt*). For you have learned that the reality of every thing is its existence, which is its luminosity (*nūrīyya*), for instance, Zayd in reality is his particular

---

1. Cf. *The Philosophy of Illumination, op. cit.*, p. 77.

existence and the light of his ipseity by which he is manifest by himself and makes other than himself [i.e. the external Zayd] manifest.

It may be asked: How could the contingent light (*al-nūr al-mumkin*) be manifest by itself when in its existence it needs the agent of existence to bestow existence and luminosity on it?

We answer: According to the definition of the Illuminationist philosophers the substantial and accidental lights (*al-anwār al-jawharīyya wa al-'araḍīyya*) are made by the simple originated making (*al-ja'al al-basīṭ al-ibdā'ī*), so the maker does not make the 'light' a light. Further, they maintain that the luminosity does not benefit that which does not have light with regard to its substance and essence (*dhāt*); rather it benefits the lights themselves and [354] makes them grow.[1] Therefore if we say 'Zayd exists', this is, according to them, analogous to our saying 'Zayd is Zayd' in a proposition that is incontrovertible, except the difference between it and our saying is 'The necessary is existent', which is a pre-eternal necessity (*ḍarūrat azalīyya*), whereas the former is essential necessity (*ḍarūrat dhātīyya*); the difference between the two necessities is explained in Logic. The contingency in the existences means the negation of pre-eternal necessity and not the negation of essential necessity. This necessity does not negate dependence on the maker-cause.

In sum, the heavens and the earth are Its particular existences and Its determined [or demarcated] lights. In reality they are lights in varying degrees and God the Exalted is the most intense degree of light and most lofty of their gradations. So 'the Light of the heavens and the earth' would be analogous to the 'Light of the lights' and the 'Sphere of the spheres'.

---

1. What is meant by 'simple originated making here' is that 'illumination is a radiated light that occurs thanks to it in the incorporeal light. It is like the illumination of the sun in that which admits of such illumination'. Cf. *The Philosophy of Illumination*, *op. cit.*, p. 98.

Since the discourse is taken according to their level, then the 'lamp' would be the similitude for the light that epiphanizes (*al-mutajalla*) on all the possible realities, and the 'niche' would stand for the lower quiddities, the 'glass' (would correspond) to the higher quiddities, the 'oil' would be the similitude for the 'breath of Mercifulness' (*al-nafas al-raḥmānī*),[1] which is the Absolute Being in His state of unfolding. This unfolding extends from the Absolute to the creation whose light-ray (*al-ḍaw*), which emanates over the moulds of things and temples (*hayākil*) of the earth and heavens in the chain of originated beginning, would be 'the most holy emanation' (*al-fayḍ al-aqdas*). The 'blessed tree' would be the 'existence' and the 'light' emanating from it would be 'the holy emanation' (*al-fayḍ al-muqaddas*)[2] that emanates [existence and light] over all things that are composed and a mixture [of elements] according to their receptacles of receptivity and their measure of preparedness in the chain of 'preparedness for the return' [to their origin]. The reason for its similitude to the tree is clear, for it consists of branches, different dimensions and plenty of twigs and small branches. This emanation is neither particular to the Orient of sheer Oneness, nor to the Occident of concrete beings and quiddities.

So the order [of the interpretation] of this verse would be as follows: The attribute of the light of Existence emanating from the Light of lights, the real Existent – the One who emanates on the contingent beings – is like the 'lamp' kindled in the 'glass' of the realities of the higher spirits and the intellectual and luminous substances by which the 'niche' of the lower substances and [355] corporeal bodies (*barāzikh* lit. isthmuses) are illuminated. The kindling of that 'lamp' is from the 'oil' of the 'breath of Mercifulness' unfolded on the degrees of existents. Because of being fine and being close to the source of good and excellence and to the mine of Light and

---

1. This term is derived from the philosophy of Ibn 'Arabī; for its meaning see *The Sufi Path of Knowledge, op. cit.*, p. 127.
2. The 'most holy emanation' and 'holy -emanation' to which Ṣadrā refers are the two major types of self-manifestation of the divine Reality in the philosophy of Ibn 'Arabī. Cf. *Sufism and Taoism* by T. Izutsu, pp. 154–157.

Existence, it emanates existence and luminosity on the things, although the fire of the 'most holy emanation' and 'holy emanation' has not touched it.

The 'oil' kindled from the 'blessed tree' that is the 'most holy emanation' is neither particular to the Orient of Oneness nor to the Occident of the concrete [existents]. This light epiphanizes on the realities of things. It is 'light upon light', because it is the necessary higher light that is the object of emanation for the inferior contingent light. 'God guides to His Light', i.e. He self-manifests His self-subsisting Existence 'to whomever He wills'. He self-manifests to someone and brings him out from the darkness of sheer non-being to the pure being of light.

This verse has other precious aspects, but its elaborate explanation will be given to you, God willing, in the course of investigation of the meanings of its words. So wait for it for seeking its lights and for harvesting its fruits.

*Excursion (*Tafrī'*)*

According to the last two aspects from these three interpretations, the [word] 'light' cannot be applied to the Necessary, the Exalted [Being] as metaphor and similitude, as the Kalām theologians of Islam and a number of exegetes of the Qur'ān have said, for the similitude of the reality to the light, or what is desired by the light here, is the Illuminator of light.

If they reflect deeply on the meaning of this derivative, they will arrive at the judgment that the Exalted is in reality the Illuminator, which entails that He is the light in reality. That is because every agent in essence having the meaning of existential perfection must have in it that meaning of perfection, for the giver of perfection cannot be deficient in it as the intuition rules and the demonstration agrees with it. If the meaning of light is found in

Him then either it is precisely the same as His essence or it is something additional to His essence. The second [assumption] would entail the dependency of the Exalted on a cause to emanate the meaning of light on Him because [356] to be attributed by something additional is the aspect of receptivity and deriving benefit, which is other than existentiation and giving benefit. If His essence is the illuminator of His essence, then it would necessitate that His essence is [both] receptive and active, in which case He will not be the simple reality. Whereas His simplicity, His oneness, His sanctity from the blemishes of all the compositions have been established, so [this assumption] will be a contradiction. Further, it would entail that His essence is more illuminating than Himself, which is impossible. If the principle of His luminosity is other than His essence, and the other than His essence is one of the contingents, then there would entail the dependence of the Necessary Being on the contingent for the attribute of perfection.

If anyone denies the light to be perfection for the existent *qua* existent, then let his mind be remedied if it has stopped [reflecting]. If he is arrogant then God will sentence him to hell, where he will abide forever. But he who contemplates on the knowledge that existence and light are united in meaning and reality but different in linguistic expression will have no doubt that existence is perfection and good for every existent *qua* existent, and the Necessary [Being] is pure existence, so He is sheer light.

It has been established and investigated that light is the very reality of the Necessary Being Himself, may His Glory be exalted.

*Section (*Faṣl*)*

The meaning of [God] relating Himself to the heavens and earth corresponds to the saying '[He is] the Light of lights', and 'the Existence of existences'. Indeed, the existence of every thing is light by which the quiddity and essence of that thing become manifest.

God is the Source of lights by His essence of light itself, and its maker (*jā'il*) by a simple making; its benefit is the derivation of the essence and the ipseity of that which is made from the essence of the Maker and His ipseity, which is precisely the same as its I-ness (*innīyya*). Accordingly, His essence is also the existentiator of the existents, the giver of will to things, and the giver of essence to essences.

Moreover, His essence being the existentiator of the essence of every contingent is nothing but the particular existence by which the quiddity is existentiated, and by which the non-being is banished from it, and is attributed by reason as 'being-existent' and 'being-the-object-of-generation' (*al-maṣdarīyya*). Presumably when it is realized [357] that the principle thing in realization is the existence of every thing that is its reality, and the quiddity is an abstracted mental state that is coloured by the colour of existence, illuminated by its light, then [it would be realized that] the existentiator of things in reality is the Existentiator of their existences, their Originator and Maker [Who originated them] by a simple origination and sacred making which is beyond composition and does not call for two things: being made and being made by it.[1]

So existentiation of things, as you have learned, is not by the attribution of the quiddity to the existence, rather it is by the origination of their existences and their bringing into being by the Exalted Principle in the manner that has already been mentioned. Hence God the Exalted is the Existence of existences. If God is the Existence of existences then for the existents there cannot be actualization but by Him, and they cannot have any ipseity (*huwīyya*) but by His ipseity.

Further, the ipseity of the Creator does not subsist by them [i.e. existents], otherwise there would be a vicious circle and also the

1. Cf. T. Izutsu, *The Concept and Reality of Existence, op. cit.,* chapter 5, pp. 99ff, where he discusses Ṣadrā's concept of principality of existence. It is the thesis that the existence is principal with respect to its quiddities or intrinsic determination (*al-māhīyya*) that is the foundation of Ṣadrā's ontological thought.

dependence of the Necessary Being on the contingent, so both [assumptions] are absurd. Therefore, the existent in reality is the Exalted Reality and none other, and anything that exists besides Him is mentally posited (*i'tibārī*) and takes its existence along with it like the apparition of a person seen in the polished mirror or the shadow that follows him. The quiddities, all of them, are analogous to mirrors in which the form of real existence is seen; their non-existence is like the non-existence of the colour [or polish] of the mirror.

It was in this sense that [Manṣūr] al-Hallāj[1] said: 'God is the source of existents'.[2] Someone else said: 'God is the existence of the heavens and the earth.' The words of al-Shiblī[3] mention that 'in the Garden there is none but God the Exalted,'[4] as if by the Garden he meant here the fundamentally real existence because He is pure Goodness and affects all. Alluding to it is the saying of Abū'l-Abbās: 'There is none in the two worlds but my Lord, and all the existents are non-existents except His existence.'[5] This supports the saying of ['Alī ibn Abī Ṭālib], the Commander of the Faithful, the Imam of the people of unification, peace be upon him: 'I would not have worshipped a Lord whom [358] I had not seen'.[6] The saying of [Muḥammad] the Seal of prophets, peace be upon him and upon his progeny, supports this [matter]: 'There is no peace for the believers without meeting God.'[7]

---

1. Ḥusayn ibn Manṣūr al-Ḥallāj is one of the most famous Ṣūfīs of Iran. Through the works of Louis Massignon, he has also become famous in the West. He was executed in Baghdad in 309/922 because he was considered a 'heretic' by the jurists of his time.
2. Cf. *Tamhīdāt* of 'Ayn al-Quḍḍāt Hamadāni (d.525/1130), p.257. Hamadānī was a Ṣūfī, philosopher and the chief judge of Hamadan in Iran. He was executed for heresy at the age of thirty-three. He is the author of works, both in Arabic and Persian. His *Tamhīdāt,* from which Ṣadrā seems to quote, is his famous work on Sufism in the Ṣūfī circles of Iran.
3. Abū Bakr al-Shiblī (d. 334/945) was an early Muslim mystic of Baghdad.
4. *Tamhīdāt, op. cit.*, p. 234.
5. *Ibid.* p. 256.
6. Cf. Kulaynī, Shaykh Muḥammad bin Ya'qūb. *Uṣūl al-Kāfī*, edited with Persian translation and commentary by Jawād Muṣtafā, vol. 1, p. 131, no. 259.
7. *Tamhīdāt, op. cit.*, pp. 70, 257.

*Wisdom [Derived from] the Throne (*Ḥikmat 'Arshīyya*)*

The existent, according to what you have heard in the well-known philosophy, is either substance or accident; both are the famous substance and accident [in philosophy]. Know that in the existence there is a real substance and a real accident, which are other than the two well-known mental realities, for the mental notions of the two belong to the kinds of quiddities and permanent archetypes (*al-a'yān al-thābitah*), which have not even smelt the fragrance of existence[1] whereas those two are from the kinds of existence.

The 'substance', as is well known, is a quiddity without existence. Its reality lies in becoming existent, i.e. united with the concept of mental existence, which is one of the general concepts that does not inhere in a substratum. In whatever sense one may take it, it is not a description for the other meaning. The 'accident' is a quiddity, which, according to its concrete existence and in its being-existent concretely, is a description for the other thing. So both are general concepts and their substrata are two mental quiddities.

The real 'substance' and 'accident': The real substance is an independent existent which is existent by its essence and ipseity; it is necessary for itself without being attached to any other thing; in its being 'it is it', and that is God the Exalted. The real accident is that which with regard to its essence and ipseity is attached to something else, is dependent on something for its substantiality, so its substantiality and its becoming essence are through another. Hence in itself disregarding the one by which it subsists is inconceivable, to say nothing of being an existent. Thus, its essence consists of that which subsists by another, and not in that it has a meaning and that meaning is something by which it is described as dependent on another which is an absolute substratum as is the case with the accident according to the famous meaning [in philosophy]; nor is it like matter as in the substantial form in the primary sense;

1. This concept has been derived by Ṣadrā from Ibn 'Arabī, cf. *Sufism and Taoism, op. cit.*, pp. 159–161.

nor [359] a form as in the matter; nor both together as in the compound of both; nor as an agent or final [cause] as in the rest of the divisions.

The Necessary [Being], exalted be His remembrance, is the real Substance in the (afore-mentioned) sense, though this name is not applied to Him, which is a naming according to 'conditionality' (*tawqīf*). Therefore this word is not applied to Him the Exalted in the most luminous divine Law (*al-shar' al-anwar*). This is the notion and meaning of what we have discussed, though in different expression.

The accident in the real sense that we mentioned is contingent existence. [This applies to] all of them, whether the contingent is a quiddity of a substance in the famous [philosophic] sense, or an accident. All those existences are accidents that subsist by the existence of the reality, but not in the sense of the subsistence of the meaning of accident by substance, as is well known among many [scholars], because that would entail that the Existence of the Exalted is the substratum for the happenings, as is maintained by some Kalām theologians, or is the substratum for the forms of knowledge, as is maintained by many Peripatetic philosophers. Rather, this is another meaning of subsistence, other than what has been said or is being said; but the expression is deficient to explain it, and the similitudes common in the language of gnostics are not apt to be struck concerning Him. In brief, the meaning of 'subsistence of things by Him the Exalted' is an expression for His self-subsistence (*qayyūmīyya*) for them. So understand, be firm and discern the intention of what is reported from Ka'b al-Aḥbār in the commentary on the word '*Allāh*'. He said: 'It is an expression for His Being and His concomitants.'[1] His concomitants are His beautiful Names and their loci of manifestation, I mean, quiddities and contingent archetypes on whose temples there occurs the effusion of the existence of the reality and the flashes and shadows of His light; the two are interpreted as 'the heavens and the earth'.

1. This explanation is taken over by Ṣadrā from *Tamhīdāt, op. cit.*, pp. 257–258.

Nearer to this meaning is that which I saw in the symbolic writings of the people of God that the root of the heaven and the earth and the reality of the two is the 'light of Muḥammad' (*nūr Muḥammad*),[1] peace be upon him and upon his progeny, and the fire of Satan (*Iblīs*), may God's curse be upon him (respectively). The explanation of this meaning will follow soon, God willing.

*Illuminative Flash (*Lam'at Ishrāqīyya*)*

You must have comprehended that light is a simple reality. Linguistically it means 'Manifest by itself, [360] making another manifest'. You must have understood from what we have said that the reality of light is manifest to someone only through the 'witnessing by presence' (*al-mushāhidah al-ḥuḍurīyya*)[2] without the representation of it in the mind. That is because every mental form is always a universal even though particularized by a thousand particular things, so it will be obscure, and anything obscure cannot be something determined and manifest in itself. If we assume that its particularization needs the bestower of particularization for its manifestation and determination then in that case its manifestation would not be identical with its essence. Therefore it would not be manifest in itself and make another manifest. Hence this [assumption] is a contradiction [to the aforementioned definition of light].

Also, anything that is not light is hidden in itself and dark in its substance; it is made manifest by the light shining on it, so how can it be the object of manifestation for the light and something that can make a thing known or unveil it!

---

1. Cf. U. Rubin, 'Pre-existence and Light: Aspects of the Concept of Nūr Muḥammad', in *Islamic Oriental Studies*, vol. V, 1995, pp. 62–119. The author has recorded this concept from both Sunnī and Shī'ite traditional sources.
2. It is a supra-conscious or above normal state of consciousness in which the object of knowledge is attained without any concept.

So know for certain that God the Exalted is manifest by His essence, because His essence is precisely the same as the manifestation of His essence for His essence, which is precisely the same as the manifestation of all things to Him. Also, He manifests them from being concealed in the loci of concealment, brings them to existence from the hiddenness of non-being to the world of being. He is the luminary by His essence, which illuminates the obscurity of quiddities, which are dark essences. Through Him the light spreads in the depth of ipseities, and the sun of His magnificence rises on the horizons of the realities of contingents, whereby the nonexistence and darkness leave from the clime of meanings [or ideas] and intelligibles. If there had not been the rise of His luminary essence in the horizons of the ipseities of contingent beings, and the illumination of His light on the heavens and the earth and what is in between them, not a single particle of existence nor any existent would have been obtained, either in the mind or concretely.

There is a tradition of the chosen Prophet, may the benedictions of God be upon its speaker and upon his most noble progeny: 'God the Exalted created the creation in darkness; then He sprinkled over them something from His light.'[1] In truth, by this (tradition) the meaning of the words of the Sublime becomes clear, that 'His Command governs the affair from the heaven to the earth' [32:5]; and His saying 'God is the great Knower of the invisible things' [9:78]. Now God's governing is precisely the same as the illumination [361] of the light of existence from Him on the things at His origination of things by way of wisdom and welfare. Likewise, His knowledge of the unseen things is precisely the same as His bringing into existence the things hidden in their essence and intelligible to Him. This bringing into existence is a kind of intellection with regard to Him, as the Illuminạtionist philosophers view it. For the existences of things are neither delayed from His desire and will for them, nor is His desire for the things, which is precisely the same as His differentiated knowledge of their existence

1. *Tamhīdāt, op. cit.* pp. 74, 256.

posterior to their existence. Rather, He existentiates the existents that are intelligible to Him, and intellects the intelligibles that are existent for Him the Exalted. So this is the meaning of 'His knowledge is action', according to them.

What is derived is: His knowledge, which is precisely the same as His essence, is the cause of the existence of the things, which consist of their being known to Him and the illumination of His light upon them. So He is God in the heaven and God in the earth. Thus from this [interpretation] also the meaning of His saying 'God is light' is unveiled.

*Assistance through Unveiling (*Ta'īd Istikshāfī*)*

The masters (*Shuyūkh*) of this spiritual path say: 'Light' means "He Who illumines the hearts of the gnostics by His unity, and enlightens the 'mysteries' (*asrār*) [1]of the loved ones by His assistance [or confirmation]".'

It is said: 'He Who gives forms to the things and light to "*asrār*".'

It is said: 'He Who guides the hearts towards the traces of the reality and to choose Him, and guides the "*asrār*" towards His supplication and choose Him.'

Indicating to this is His saying 'God is the Friend of those who believe, He brings them out from the darkness to the light' [2:257]. That means [He brings them out], from the unreality to the reality, from the servant to the Lord, from the distance to the closeness [to the Lord], from the lower [plenum] to the higher [plenum], from the abyss [of hell] to the Gardens.

---

1. By '*asrār*' (sing. '*sirr*'), Ṣadrā means the level of being of man which is higher than the spirit. According to gnostics, from whom he quotes, the being of man has seven principal levels, and they are in the ascending order: nature (*ṭab'*), soul (*nafs*), reason (*'aql*), spirit (*rūḥ*), mystery (*sirr*), hidden (*khafī*), most hidden (*akhfā'*). Cf., his '*Tafsīr sūrah al-Ḥadīd*' in *Tafsīr al-Qur'ān al-Karīm*, vol. 6, p. 23, etc.

*Fiery Unveiling (*Kashf Istinārī*)*

Know that the Exalted Reality has contrary names that are inherent in His essence, such as the First (*al-awwal*) and the Last (*al-ākhir*), the Manifest (*al-ẓāhir*) [362] and the Hidden (*al-bāṭin*), the Guide (*al-hādī*) and the Misguider (*al-muḍil*), the Giver of might (*al-mu'izz*)and the Giver of disgrace (*al-mudhil*). So according to His necessary existential Unity He has Attributes from the two contrary Attributes. The eminent of the two pertains to the beauty of His Essence and the embellishment of His Face. Its contrary aspect is attested to Him in comparison to the greatness of His Essence and His Majesty to that which is below Him, and to His domination on another. Hence the Names and Attributes of Beauty are affirmed for Him first and by essence, and the Names and Attributes of Majesty are attested to Him next and by accident as something incontrovertible, as is mentioned in the discussion on the final cause which is the active agent for the activity of the agent.

By this principle the rule 'It is impossible for the good in reality to be the source of evils' is preserved. By this [rule] Aristotle, the master of philosophers and foremost among the Peripatetic philosophers, banished the doubt of those such as the Dualists who maintained the plurality in the First Agent of all. Now every contingent is a dual in reality, consisting of an aspect of the luminous perfection emerging from the luminous Attributes of [divine] Beauty and an aspect of the imperfection of the tenebrous non-being emerging from the dominating fiery Attributes of [divine] Majesty. From these two aspects there emerges the Muḥammadan light and the Satanic fire (respectively), [the former] pervading the heavens of the spirits and spiritual beings and the [latter] pervading the earth of corporeal bodies and corporeal things.

God the Exalted is the illuminator of all by the light of His existence and beauty, and by the fire of His awe and majesty, to which He alluded in His words 'God is the Friend of those who believe, He brings them out from the darkness to the light' [2:257].

So God is the light of the heavens and the earth through the lights of the stars of His beautiful Names of light shining in the sky of the reality of His essence. The rays of the luminary substances are in the horizons of His celestial world [or the world of Soul] and in His world of Intellects (*Jabarūt*, lit. Omnipotence). All the existents are subjugated to these two Attributes, constantly fluctuating between the two fingers [of God]. The Throne and what it encompasses is between the two Attributes from the Attributes of the Sublime; the heart and what attracts it is between the two fingers of the fingers of the Most Merciful, which are the two degrees of the two Attributes of gentleness and dominance. In the other station they are the two substances, intellect and soul, yet at another level they are the two [spiritual] states of expansion and contraction.

The shadows of the two in the universe are the heaven and the earth; in the stars there are those of good fortune and those of ill omen; [363] in the horizons there is the orient and the occident; in the animals male and female; in the foods sweet and bitter; in the colour black and white; in the quantity that which is joined and that which is disjointed; in the measure there is that which is stable and that which is unstable; in the line there is the straight line and there is the curved line; in the plane there is the flat plane and there is the curved plane; in the number there is odd and even; in the school of law (*madhhab*) there is guidance and misguidance; in belief there is truth and falsehood; in the soul there is advancing and retreating; in the heart there is insight and blindness; in the next world there is the bliss [of Garden] and the torment of hell; in this world there is fortune and misfortune; in the inner being of man there is inspiration and [devilish] whispering, etc. from the formation of pairs pervading in every atom (*dharārī*), descending from the heaven of the universe of unity to the earth of the universe of multiplicity and matter, as [is given] in the saying of the Exalted: 'Of everything We have created pairs' [51:49].

There are very few learned scholars (*al-'ulamā'*) who have given the explanation of the details of these paired degrees, descending from the eminence of the heaven of loftiness and greatness to the perigee of the lowly earth, then ascending to the world of [divine] Names and Great Resurrection in which the things will gather towards the Exalted Lord, for 'all of them come alone on the Day of Resurrection' [19:95].

[The Second] Chapter

His saying, may His name be glorified:

> The similitude of His Light is that of a lamp in a niche,
> the lamp is in a glass;
> the glass is like a glittering star.
> (*mathalu nūrihi ka-mishkātin fīhā misbāhun; al-misbāhu fī zujājatin; al-zujājatu ka-annahā kawkabun durriyun*)

Praise be to the worshipper who has reached in his servitude and wayfaring on the spiritual path of deputyship [leading] the station of being a witness to the light of the Face of God by the witnessing of the heart, and sees it as he sees by the physical vision the light of the lamp from behind the glass situated in the niche. That which corresponds to the glass of this light [364] is Muḥammad the Messenger of God, may peace be upon him and upon his progeny. For it is not possible to witness the light of Divine Unity owing to its great intensity and power, which subjugates the insights and overwhelms the reasons except from behind the veil of the Muḥammadan glass, for it is through him that the lamp of light of the Sublime is recognized before the dawn of its manifestation.

If you wish to relate the lamp to the light and the morning to the manifestation, then say: 'He is God, the One' [112:1]. Your saying,

'He is God (*huwa Allāh*)' consists of two words, subject and predicate. The predicate is a kind of unification of the essence and existence; but if you relfect logically on the condition of this predicate you will find 'He is God' is one thing and one essence. The two are sometimes expressed as Necessary Being and Unity of Essence (*al-dhāt al-aḥadīyya*), and sometimes as inclusive of all the Attributes of perfection and beautiful Names.

The object of denotation of the two aforementioned modes is one simple reality, which according to one aspect is Ipseity and according to the other the Divinity, as He is Existence according to one consideration, and Name and Attribute according to another consideration.[1] Just as the lamp in the realm of physical vision is one thing and one sensory object but upon analysis it is divided into two things, one is the light, which corresponds to the Absolute Existence, and the [other] is the pine-shaped [lamp], the substratum [of the light] that corresponds to the meaning [or notion] of the name 'Allah' of the Exalted Necessary [Being].

This is so if 'the glass' is taken as a symbol for 'God the Exalted', but if it is [taken for] a contingent essence like the essence of the Messenger, peace be upon him and upon his progeny, then one thing will correspond to existence and the second to quiddity in the contingent being.

There is a difference in the three positions: The attribute and the attributed in the lamp, that is the light and pine-shaped lamp, are united in sensory [perception] and in position, but can be differentiated mentally and in existence. Analogous to these two in the contingent being are the quiddity and existence, which are united in existence and concretely, differentiated mentally and in naming. In the case of the Exalted Necessary Being, that which corresponds to existence in contingent being and luminosity in [365] the lamp is called 'ipseity'. It is precisely the same as the name

1. This very concept is also derived from the metaphysics of Ibn 'Arabī, cf. *The Sufi Path of Knowledge, op. cit.*, pp. 36–37.

'Allāh', which corresponds to quiddity [in the contingent] and the substratum of flame [in the lamp]. There is no difference [between the Absolute Being and Allāh] except in expression. So the lamp is a symbol for 'Allah' and its light is a symbol for the Unity of Ipseity (*al-huwīyya al-aḥadīyya*) [of His Being].

If the light of the lamp did not have a substratum having the determination of position, then there would not be the particularization of the dimension of proximity and distance from it in the air from which strength and weakness [of light] is illuminated. Then the light from it would not fall on a thing from the air of the house, its walls and its roof because of the absence of a relation with the preponderance and its nonexistence, the non-existence of priority, and the impossibility of the preponderance without a preponderator.

Likewise, if the reality had no names from which the particular effects occur on the loci of manifestation and the loci of its epiphany according to what is requisite of the self-determination of every Name from the other Name, then there would not generate (*ṣudūr*) from it anything from the contingents in the world of existence, because there would be no priority for any contingent, nor preponderance for it over the other contingent from the aspect of the dimension of contingency. The contingent quiddities and the universal meanings do not exist on one level according to the essence in receptivity and non-receptivity of the light of Existence. Rather, the one that determines a special station and a determined level for all of them is the Essence of the Necessary Being according to what is necessary for them from the Names and Attributes emerging from the reality of divine Ipseity, the sun of the Necessary Reality, the one who penetrates its light in all the temples of contingent beings, who spreads its emanation over the plain of all the quiddities.

The first one who knocked at the door of illumination by the light of God, and the first one who spoke 'There is no god but God' is the exalted servant, the First Intellect, the eminent contingent, the 'reality' of Muḥammad (*al-ḥaqīqah al-Muḥammadīyya*).[1] He is the lamp of the light of God, the one who emanates the light of goodness and munificence. Through his medium all the quiddities situated in the expanse of receptivity to existence and ipseities, dwelling in the atmosphere of the houses of the people of love and servitude to the Originator, of existence receive the emanation and light. So the essence of the Prophet, peace be upon him and upon his progeny, was like the polished mirror before the Face of the greatest Luminary and was parallel to the reality, hence the Face of the Lord possessing Majesty and Generosity epiphanized in it.

*Excursion (*Tafrī'*)*

[366] When any one among the indigents of his community, previous and subsequent, straightens his relation with him then there reflects on him the light of the reality through him, peace be upon him and upon his progeny. This is the meaning of 'intercession' (*al-shafā'ah*), which all people need, even the prophets and friends [of God], preceding and subsequent, on the Day of Resurrection when 'some faces on that day shall be radiant, gazing at their Lord' [75:22–23].

Know that the original purpose of worships (*'ibādāt*) and spiritual disciplines is the cleansing of the surface of [man's] essence by the purified hearts and facing towards the light of the reality behind the 'glass' of Muḥammad, peace be upon him and upon his family, in order to witness the light of God. Then the luminous ray of knowledge of God may fall on him. This is the meaning of what

1. By the 'reality of Muḥammad', Ṣadrā means the 'spirit' of Prophet Muḥammad. According to his notion the Prophet's 'reality' or 'spirit' was united with the First Intellect, hence it was pre-eternal from the aspect of reality and temporal from the aspect of being human. Cf. his '*Tafsīr Āyat al-kursī*', in *Tafsīr al-Qur'ān al-Karīm*, vol. 4, p. 131.

Uways al-Qaranī,[1] may God be pleased with him, said, that 'the servant's life must be like the life of his Lord' and what we have mentioned refers in sum to the meaning of 'perfect servanthood'.

A certain 'possessor of the heart' was asked: 'What is the perfect servanthood?' He replied: 'If you become free then you become a servant.' It means, if you become disengaged and liberated from attachments [to appetites], and your heart is purified from impurities [of the soul], then you become a servant of God, a proximate angel, a king and owner of everything by the might, power and sovereignty of God. 'Certainly God conferred a benefit upon believers when He raised among them a Messenger from among themselves' [3:164].

This meaning is also recorded from the Messenger of God, may peace be upon him and upon his progeny, regarding the report about the inhabitants of the Garden: 'An angel approaches them after asking for their permission to enter. When he has entered he presents them with a letter from God. In the letter He had addressed every human being as 'From the Eternal Living One to the eternal Living One. As for the contents: In truth I say to a thing: Be, and it is [16: 40]. Behold, today I make you someone who can say to a thing: Be, and it is'. He, peace be upon him and upon his progeny, commented: 'That is why if anyone from the inhabitants of Garden say to a thing, "Be", it just is.'

*Admonition (*Tanbīh*)*

[367] O, indigent one, it is necessary for you to learn the distinction between the mirror and the person, and to differentiate between the shadow and him who casts the shadow. We have already exhorted

1. Uways al-Qaranī was a contemporary of Prophet Muḥammad who is supposed to have lived in Yemen but never met the Prophet. The Islamic tradition relates that he spent all his nights in prayers. For the later Ṣūfīs he became the prototype of the inspired Ṣūfī who was guided solely by God without the outer connection with the Prophet.

earlier that there should not happen to you what has (happened to) many people gone astray and driven back, and those who maintained the incarnation and the physical embodiment of the divine. For what is the worth of dust before the Lord of the lords, 'you did not throw when you threw but God threw' [8:17]. [Muḥammad] the master of the pious ones, the leader of the virtuous ones, peace be upon him and upon his progeny, was addressed by His word, 'surely you cannot guide whom you love [but God guides whom He wills]' [28:56]. So what would be [the worth] of those of your like and your type!

This degree is expressed as 'the trust' (*al-amānah*) in His saying: 'We did indeed offer the trust to the heavens, the earth and the mountains, but they refused to carry it and were afraid of it, but man carried it. He has, indeed, been unjust and ignorant' [33:72]. In this (saying) there are subtle insights mentioned earlier. The 'trust' [in the end] is entrusted to its owner. Now, every quality pertaining to existence and the perfection pertaining to light emanated by God on one of the contingents and on one of the quiddities is a trust from God with him.[1] He has but to become coloured by His light, to be in His vicinity and surrounded by Him and not [just] be attributed by His reality. That is why he is divested of [everything] at the giving up of the 'trusts' so all return to Him, for 'unto God all things come home' [42:53].

It is to this meaning that Abū Sa'īd al-Kharrāz[2] alluded when he said: 'The mark of the disciple in [the state of] annihilation is that his share from this world and the next world goes except that from God the Sublime; then that also begins to annihilate, and he sees the

1. The term *al-amānah* (trust) has been interpreted in a number of commentaries on the Qur'ān as 'contract or transaction' (*'aqd*), 'task' (*taklīf*), 'obedience' (*al-ṭā'ah*), etc. Ṣadrā interprets it as 'existence'. He gives thi interpretation clearly in one of his short treatises in Arabic in *The Complete Philosophical Treatises of Ṣadr al-Dīn Muḥammad al-Shīrāzī*, edited by Ḥ. N. Isfahānī, p. 361.
2. Abū Sa'īd Aḥmad al-Kharrāz (d.277 or 287/890 or 899) was one of the early Ṣūfīs and probably the master of Junayd Abū'l-Qāsim Muḥammad (d. 297/909), who was one of the foremost Ṣūfīs of the school of Baghdad.

existence of his ego-consciousness and his share of seeing God also annihilating, and there remains from his seeing what was for God from God; so the servant becomes singular by His singularity. If that is so then there is not with God other than God, and God remains the One, the Eternal in post-eternity as He was in pre-eternity.' This is what he said. It is perfect in its meaning for the one who has the ear to hear His signs, and the intellect to comprehend His unity, the eye to see [368] His power and the penetration of His command in the physical and celestial worlds, in the seen and the unseen [realms].

*Another Way [of Admonition] (*Ṭarīq Ākhir*)*

It is reported from some earlier exegete [of the Qur'ān] that, 'niche' symbolizes [man's] breast, 'glass' the heart and 'lamp' the spirit. This perception is obvious and clear, but it must be learned that each of these three, namely, the breast, the heart and the spirit, has three levels. The first one is evident and clear to everyone because of being from the realm of exterior senses; the second one is hidden from the external senses, unveiled to the interior senses; the third one is hidden from both altogether, unveiled to the theoretical intellect (*al-'aql al-naẓarī*). It has other degrees as well but this is not the place to explain that.

The first level is that of the breast. It is composed of bones, membranes, bundles [of nerves], which are surrounded by the mass of liver. By that it is meant either the liver thanks to its being the substratum of the natural spirit (*al-rūḥ al-ṭabī'ī*), or the heart, which is the pine-shaped flesh, or the spirit, which is a warm, subtle body and the mount of the animal soul, the perceiver of the particulars for the sake of concupiscent and irascible motions.

Now we come to the second level of each. The breast denotes the natural spirit; the heart, as already mentioned, the animal spirit; and the spirit the psychic human spirit which is connected to it. The human cogitative soul uses it for the objectives pertaining to [its] animal life and for deliberation on the management of [matters] pertaining to [its] human life with regard to its living and Return, for this world and the next world according to the requisite of the practical intellect that is common in mankind. Both the common and elite agree that in it lies his getting rid of obstacles and [evil] whisperings, and its safety from alienations and disputes.

[369] These three spirits, i.e. natural, animal (or vital) and psychic, are the ones that physicians investigate. They are named 'spirits' by them, and are distinguished by them by three definitions. Their hierarchical difference in their being-body, in strength and weakness in the subtlety and in the perfection and imperfection in balance. Each of them has a particular place of birth and origin. The [place of] origin of the psychic spirit is the brain. This is the most balanced spirit. The place of origin of the animal spirit is the pine-shaped heart. It is average in the perfection of balance. The birthplace of the natural spirit is the liver; which is further away from the balance. These three spirits are the most eminent elemental bodies, so much so that they almost resemble the spheres. According to the gnostics their names are what we have already mentioned, i.e. breast, heart and spirit. So according to this usage they hold an intermediary level.

The third level is as follows. The breast according to this level stands for the animal soul, which the human heart uses. At this station it is an expression for the rational soul (*al-nafs al-nāṭiqah*) and the practical intellect (*al-'aql 'amalī*), as already mentioned. The spirit is an expression for the acquired intellect (*al-'aql al-mustafād*), the one that witnesses the intelligibles at its contact with the Active Intellect (*al-'aql al-fa''āl*), which is the holy angel (*al-malak al-muqaddas*) – the pen of God, which writes the realities of faith on the tablets of our hearts, as the Exalted said: 'Recite and your Lord is the Most Bounteous, Who taught by the pen, taught man that which he knew not' [96:3–5].

These three in the last level are from the next world – the invisible, celestial world. In the first level they are from this world – the visible, manifest world. In the intermediary level they are placed in between the two worlds as an isthmus between the two configurations, which corresponds to the world of spheres. It is said that it is '*al-a'rāf*' (the elevated place) [7:46].

The heart according to the last meaning is called the 'Throne of God' and the 'Seat' of the Divine Name Most Merciful (*al-raḥmān*) because of being the substratum for the knowledge of God and His kingdom, and in being upright without twisting or [370] deviating in the magnificence of His Essence, Attributes, Names, Acts, Books, messengers and the Last Day, which is the Day of the Return of the creatures to Him and of the coming back of the spirits and their imaginary bodies (*muthūl*) before Him.

The breast is the Footstool. The relation of the Throne to the Footstool is like the relation of the Intellect to the Soul, the Decree (*al-qaḍā'*) to the Allotment (*al-qadar*). For all the intelligibles are undifferentiated in the Decree, differentiated in the Allotment. Likewise, the starry lights are connected together as one in the Throne thanks to its utmost purity and subtlety and its having affinity with the horizonof the realm of meaning and celestial kingdom. But they are differentiated and diversified in the Footstool because the stars in subtlety are lower than the sphere of the Throne.

[The Third] Chapter

His saying:

> Kindled from a blessed tree, an olive
> that is neither of the Orient nor of the Occident.
> (*Yūqadu min shajaratin mubārakatin zaytūnatin lā sharqīyya wa lā gharbīyya*)

Know that this tree is not from the trees of this world – the realm of sense – as those who are veiled [from the real meaning] surmise, otherwise it would have been in a part of the world that is capable of sensory indication. But that is not the case. So it is not in this world. But it is not in the other world either, as is the view of another group.

Ḥasan al-Baṣrī[1] said: 'If this tree was in this world then either it would pertain to the Orient or to the Occident; but by God it is neither in this world nor in the Garden [of the next world]. It is a symbol which God has struck for His light.'[2]

At times one thing has many names according to different considerations, but the objective in all is one meaning, though the

1. Ḥasan al-Baṣrī (d. 110/728) was an early Ṣūfī ascetic of Iraq.
2. *Tamhīdāt, op. cit.*, p. 263.

words could be many and aspects multiple. At times one reality has different levels in the worlds, which are parallel, mutually connected; some are above the other, like the heart whose manifest [aspect] is the body composed of four elements; then it is a mixture of [371] the four (humours), then the mixture of blood and water such as fat, flesh, nerves, blood vessels and the like. The exterior of its manifest form is the sensible, pine-shaped red form, the interior of its manifest form is a tenebrous, dark cavity; its interior is the vaporous spirit derived from the subtle [matter] of the mixture and their vapours, its exterior is derived from the gross [matter] of the mixture and its earthly nature. The relation of the latter to the former is like the relation of the earth to the sky.

Its interior has an interior and that is the animal soul, which is an exterior shell to the intellectual human soul. Its relation to this (human) soul is like the relation of the body to it. Then for the interior of its interior there is another interior. All these, as mentioned earlier, are shells in relation to it, and it encompasses them, [like] the Throne encompassing everything in it from the heaven and the earth (*farsh*). And this is an intellectual substance that emanates from the soul from the Active Principle. At the beginning of its generation (*takawwun*) it corresponds to the mental meanings and material universal notions [or its material intellect]. Its relation to the Active Intellect is like the relation of semen to man.

Then it progresses in the power of intellectual existence to the level of intellect *in habitus* (*al-'aql bi'il-malakah*) by which it perceives the primary premises, comprehends the associative and disparate [ideas], discerns the concepts and judgments derived from the sense-perceptions; then to the level of intellect in act (*al-'aql bi'l-fi'l*) by which it perceives the [rational] inquiries, the definitions of quiddities, the demonstrations of the existents; then to the level of acquired intellect, where it witnesses the forms of intelligibles in the Higher Pen, and the Preserved Tablet (*al-lawḥ al-maḥfūẓ*); then it joins the proximate angels and unites with them, a unity which is of light, sanctified from the blemishes of deficiency and imperfection. All these are among the totality of the degrees of human heart in its ascent from the earth of corporeal body to the heaven of the Divine Names and Attributes (*al-samā' al-lāhūtīyya*).

Thus on the basis [of the above interpretation] the words in this verse employed by the people of *Sharī'ah* in general and the people of spiritual reality (*ahl al-ḥaqīqah*) in particular could be compared with other than these realities. The 'olive tree', according to the people who are veiled [from the spiritual realities] [372], limited to the first level of realities and the lowest realm of spiritual meanings, is a tree that grows in Shām [i.e. the present Palestine, Jordan, Syria and Lebanon] and other [places]. The most excellent quality of olive is the olive of Shām. It is blessed because it has many benefits, or because it is firm in the earth, which is blessed [by God] for the people, or there is bliss in it because the bodies of seventy of the prophets including Abraham, peace be upon them, are buried in it.

The Prophet, peace be upon him and upon his progeny, is reported to have said: 'For you is this tree; use the oil of olive for the treatment of ulcers for it cures them.'

Its place of growth is neither in the Orient nor in the Occident, for Shām is in the middle of the Orient and Occident of the world, i.e. in one fourth of the earth manifest from the ocean which is on one of its two sides. In length it is half of the great circle of the earth. The Khālidāt islands are situated on the Occidental side. They surfaced from the ocean in ancient times but now they are submerged in it. The other side ends at the construction near the shore of the ocean on the side of the Orient.

It is said: [This tree] is not in a place where the sun always shines on it, nor in a place where the sun never shines on it, but [in a place] where the sun and the shadow follow each other on it, and that (is why) it is excellent in bearing [fruit], and most refined in its oil. The Messenger of God, peace be upon him, said: 'There is no good in a tree on which the sun never shines, nor in the vegetation on which the sun never shines, nor is there any good in them if they are always in the sunshine.'

From these two views it is derived that it is a tree situated on the horizon of the dome of the earth. This in the technical terminology of the astronomers is a place of the earth whose length is ninety degrees, its breadth is the breadth of the middle of the climes, or half of a quarter of a circle, I mean, forty-five degrees. According to the first view it has a central position in the length between the rising and the setting of the sun in the populated earth. According to the second view it is medium in width and is situated between the height of the rising of the sun in the long midday and its ultimate perigee in the inhabited places; or the day in it becomes median between very long and very short throughout the [373] year, like the places situated in the equator and below it.

This explanation of the notion of 'olive tree' accordingly has been arrived at by the observation of many according to its appearance in the places of this world and its existence in the abyss of dense bodies and dark mines. But its investigation according to the second mode of existence (*nash'at ukhrā*) is other than this mode of existence (*nash'at*). Different Qur'ānic allusions and prophetic symbols are given to it according to the stations of the gnostics and the levels of those who remember [God] (*al-mutadhakkirūn*). Sometimes it is expressed as the 'Tūbā Tree'[13:29]; sometimes as the 'Lot Tree' (*sidrat al-muntahā'*) [53:15] before it is the Garden of Refuge [53:15]; sometimes the station of 'I stayed in the house with my Lord Who fed me and gave me water;'[1] sometimes as the 'Tree of Moses', 'a tree springing out from Mount Sinai, that produces oil and is seasoning for the eaters' [23:20]. This 'oil' is of the illuminating demonstrative objectives of knowledge and the seasoning of addresses and beautiful sermons acceptable to the reasons striving to know.

1. Cf. *Aḥādīth-i Mathnawī*, no. 244.

[The Third] Chapter

*The Earthly Shadow in which is the Illumination from the Throne (*Taẓlīl Farshī fīhi Tanwīr 'Arshī*)*

What has reached your ears has been explained to you, that the human faculty (*quwwah*) whose first mode of existence is generated in the fleshy heart, the pine-shaped cone in position, constitutes different levels in ascension to perfection and has many developments in states. This is clear when you consider first the heart and its states. In reality it is the first organ that is generated in the body and is perpetually in motion, and the last organ to decompose and become silent. Rather, it is the animal body in reality which the soul uses through the subtle spirit that rises from it, and the rest of the organs are added because of it and are born to protect it. That is because they correspond to the protective coverings and shells for the kernel heart. The instruments [or the faculties of sense-perceptions] are servants to it, and safeguard it. That is why it is situated at the centre of the body. Though in form it is surrounded by them, and in quantity it is smaller than them, in potentiality and 'meaning' (*al-ma'nī*) it encompasses them, [374] uses them, is the goal of their existence and the donor agent for their powers.

Further, the subtle vapour is born from it, which physicians [call] the 'animal spirit' (*al-rūḥ haywānī*). Then another vaporous spirit subtler than [the former] is born from it. This is the 'psychic spirit' (*al-rūḥ nafsānī*). Then vegetal soul (*al-nafs al- nabātī*) is born from it. This is a faculty and principle for feeding, growth and reproduction, and then the animal soul. Its first degree is the tactile faculty, as is found in worms, snails and the insects of the types that have no heads. Then the sentient souls (*al-nufūs al-ḥissīyya*) of various levels are born [from the vegetal soul]; then the imaginative souls (*al-nufūs al-khayālīyya*) of various degrees; then the estimative souls (*al-nufūs al-wahmānīyya*) [of various levels]. The latter is the highest level in the animal soul *qua* animal soul. Then the angelic rational soul (*al-nafs al-nāṭiqah al-malakīyya*) comes into being. It is a light from the spiritual lights of God, which rises from the horizon of the next world. It is the first knocking at the threshold of the celestial world (*al-malakūt*). Its first level is the material intellect (*al-'aql al-hayūlānī*), which is the seed of the tree of intellect and gnosis (*'irfān*) and the grain of the fruit of gnosis and faith. Then the intellect having preparedness [to receive forms, also called intellect *in habitus*] comes into being from it; then the intellect in act; then the acquired [intellect], the illuminator of [the way to] the Place of Return (*al-Ma'ād*); then the Active Intellect for [the perception of] intelligibles, lights and emanations for the existence of realities and mysteries.

Now you have learned about the degrees of man, his journey, his travelling in the levels of [his] body, soul and intellect till he reaches the highest goals in ascension from which he descended. Then know this concerning the degrees of that from which he feeds and gets strength, becomes perfect and develops. He has in each station remedy and particular nourishments, determined associations, known pairs, some from the [domain of] bodies and physical matters, some from [the domain of] senses and sensibles, some from estimations, imaginations, surmises and beliefs, some from the intellects and intelligibles, and some from the spiritual witnessing (*al-shuhūd*) and spiritual visions (*al-mushāhidāt*).

As long as man is in the realm of this world and corporeality, he must have nourishment which resembles the feeding agent, in [375] form, matter and power [or strength]. He feeds [this] form by the form, the matter by the matter, the power by the power, and the senses by the sensibles. Further, for every organ there is a share from the nourishment which resembles and represents it after it has gone through the degrees of ripening and transmutation by the faculty of feeding. This in the body corresponds to the faculty of intellection in the soul. He must also have the nourishment of knowledge and intellectual matters for the substantiality of his soul and its essence.

Don't you see that when the food substance enters the body and presents before the management of the [faculty of] feeding, it disposes of it, transmutes it for the digestion by its powers, which are subservient [to it] for this affair. Then it cleanses it from the wastes by its natural art which resembles the art of alchemy; then it purifies it from the stains of admixture of weeds and impurity into something clean without any husks, through the four stages of digestion and transmutation. One of them is in the intestine. It extracts and separates wastes and admixtures from the [food] by this process and the exercise of warmth, which resembles the torture and heat of hell [for the evil-doers who are tortured] by the powers of the guards of hell who 'are nineteen above it' [74:30], to which [i.e. to hell] He says: 'Are you filled?' And it replies: 'Are there any more [to come]? [50:30]. Prior to that it had turned away from obedience to God and distanced [itself] from the realm of balance and unity, deviated from the road that was the straight path and strayed from the natural course (*sharī'ah*) that regulates the bodies according to the way of wisdom. When these powers become free from their service that is particular to them for this hidden traveller in this station, and it ascends a little from this dark bottomless pit [i.e. the intestine] to the other level above it, it falls into the hands of the other powers of this kind. They act on it according to what they have been commanded. Then for a second time it gets digested in the liver, and some of the residue of the waste falls from it, so it becomes a mixture of four; some do good, others do evil to [make] it emerge from its complete rejection of obedience and to bring it near to [its] welfare and servitude to the command of God which works for it in the edifice of the 'frequented house of God'.

Then these four friends become more adjusted [to each other in] the substance called blood. When it flows [376] in the blood vessels, and the perspiration emerges from it, then it has become disciplined and trodden the path of obedience to the soul. Now it occupies [itself] in the abode of the heart for the natural rites, and abides upright for a while for bodily worship. It is sound now because it wears the garb of bodily form by the hand of the form-making faculty, and is grateful for this great corporeal blessing. Then a remnant from the unwanted appendage is taken by the hands of the faculty of reproduction so that it becomes matter for another body like it in species.

Now that you have learned how the state of the perfection of the body is completed, what increases it in measure and power to the highest point of perfection then know that likewise the state of perfection of the soul lies in psychic and intellectual food. The soul by its perceptive power brings a sensible form to its presence. At the beginning it disposes (*taṣarruf*) in it by the governing faculty (*al-quwwah al-mutaṣarrifah*), that is, it separates it from the dross of matter which is like the primal waste for the food, or like the deep pit (*hāwīyah*) for the people deserving punishment and retribution [in the next world]. This act from the soul is called 'sensation'. This is the active operation (or disposal) by the soul, and the passive perfection for the senses.

Then the (soul) exercises another operative action on that form, and that is once again separating it from the (remaining) peels in the most complete way, until the material covering is removed from it. This is called 'imagination' (*al-takhyīl*) and 'representation' (*al-taṣwīr*). The form at this point has become perfect nourishment for the imaginative faculty. Its relation to (the faculty of imagination) is as the relation of the sensible to the sense.

The (soul) further executes another action over [the form], that is, removing from it the matter and all its accidents. Yet, whenever it is related to a particular matter, it still has a sort of attachment to the matter. This (action) is called 'estimation' (*al-tawahhum*). Further, if it performs another action over the form [right after its act of estimation], then it denudes it from all the traces of the matter and its accidents, as well as its attachments and affiliations, so it becomes a pure kernel, quite intelligible to the innermost intellect, which is one of the angels of God, because it has become completely purified from all its material errors and shortcomings and [377] sensible sins. It asks for forgiveness [from God], and turns [to Him] and repents, and returns and comes back to Him, and 'the one who repents of the sin is like the one who has no sin'. So reflect on the wisdom of the Creator, how He originated a faculty of intellect, which performs an activity on the sensible and renders it intelligible (*ma'qūl*) and comprehensible (*'āqil*).

From what we have mentioned it is learned that for every thing there is a particular natural course leading to the ultimate good and highest goal; so every lower thing travels towards the high, and everything high has mercy and providence (*'ināyah*) for the low, which resembles the First Principle in emanating all goodness.

Also, it is learned that food is like the subject who feeds it; it develops in various levels, and at each level it is named and known by a particular name that relates to [that level]. Its lowest way-station and the most inferior one is the element; then after its transformations it turns into a composite mineral body like grain, bread or olive. Then after [traversing] the degrees of regulations it becomes blood and a sound mixture. Soon after, it becomes flesh, cartilage and nerves; then a warm subtle vapour. Afterwards it becomes a sentient and sensible form; then an imaginative form; then an estimative or intellective form; then it ascends to the level of witnessing the divine lights and seeing the divine Attributes (*al-ṣifāt al-lāhūtīyya*) and the Lordly Names. According to each level pertaining to the world of Creation (*al-khalqīyya*) and the world of Command (*al-amrīyya*), and according to every garment of light and darkness [it wears] and removes it has a specific name.

God has struck a similitude for the believer, his levels in the knowledge and the elevation towards Him till he becomes 'light upon light' to the 'olive tree'; his elevation to the utmost perfection and his wayfaring according to the [divine] guidance to the 'sensible light'; and his arriving before Him to the 'light upon light'.

So the 'olive tree' corresponds to the plant producing the fruit whose taste is delicate for the perfect man [378] who is the noblest creation of God and His servant going towards His Lord, like Khalīl [i.e. the prophet Abraham], peace be upon him, when he said, 'I am going to my Lord Who will guide me' [37:99], and like Moses, peace be upon him, when he said, 'I observe a fire' [20:10], and like our Prophet, peace be upon him and upon his progeny, when he said, 'Glory be to Him Who carried His servant by night from the Mosque' [17:1].

The 'olive' corresponds to the food and nourishment that man eats and makes it enter in his abdomen. The 'niche' stands for the human body on account of being tenebrous in its essence and receptive to the light in an uneven manner owing to the differences of the surface and perforation in it. So is the case with the human body, which is not equal in its reception to the sensible lights and motions.

The 'glass' stands for the heart with regard to its cavity, which is a place for the animal spirit which corresponds to the 'fat of the oil'.

The 'lamp' (corresponds) to the psychic spirit enlightened by the light of the human soul. This spirit, owing to its greatest proximity to the invisible, celestial world, is 'like the oil, which would shine even if no fire touched it' from the outside. This is because the essential causes (*al-'ilal al-dhātīyya*) are not the affairs external to the essences of the caused ones (*dhawāt al-ma'alūlāt*). The [psychic spirit] which receives the light of the [human] soul though it is in need of being illuminated by the Active Intellect, still it does not need a cause external to its essence [for being illuminated], so it is as if self-sufficient in its essence of the [external] cause.

As for the description of the 'glass' that it is 'a glittering star', that is because the heart in reality is its cavity, which is filled with the light of animal spirit and illuminated by it.

[This spirit] is 'kindled from a blessed tree' because the matter of its spirit is from the nourishing trees and plants full of blessings for obtaining the spirits, their souls and intellects after numerous transformations and movements, just as the oil is obtained from the olives after forceful pressings.

[379] As for the description of the tree that it is 'neither of the Orient nor of the Occident', it means: the most delicate food and most balanced mixture is in the country and place that is in the middle of the unveiled quarter of the earth, as mentioned earlier.

*Sacred Section (*Faṣl Taqdīsī*)*

That was the interpretation of the Light Verse with respect to the domain of the human body, which is the corporeal microcosm. It has two other interpretations: one pertains to the realm of horizons and the other to the realm of souls.

First: the 'niche' stands for the world of corporeal bodies; the 'glass' (is the similitude) for the Throne; the 'lamp' (corresponds to) the Great Spirit; the 'tree' stands for the universal matter which is the matter for the realities of the corporeal bodies, and its variegated forms correspond to the branches and leaves. It [i.e. the universal matter] in itself is something celestial and intellectual except that it is most low and most inferior among the celestial substances. It is the end of the world of spirits and the beginning of the world of corporeal bodies. So it can neither be related to the Orient of the world of Intellects and Spirits nor to the Occident of the world of corporeal bodies and apparitions. 'Its oil whereof', that is, (the oil) of the realm of the psychic spirits, 'would shine' by the lights of the Active Intellects, 'even if no fire touched it'. [The fire] stands for the light of the eternal power [which 'would shine'] because of the proximity of its nature to the existence. 'Light upon light', the first light stands for the light of divine Mercy and Lordly gnosis, the second light stands for the light of the Exalted Spirit and the Active Intellect; also the former is the light of the Active Intellect and the latter is the light of the Universal Soul (*al-nafs al-kullīyya*), which is the light of the Throne – the seat of the compassionate noetic light of mercifulness. It is like the Form of the All Merciful so it becomes 'light upon light', as in His saying, 'The All Merciful sat upon the Throne' [20:5]. 'God guides to His light whom He wills' [24:35] is an allusion to the emanation of the light of Mercifulness, which is divided among everyone who desires God. Its existentiation is from the Throne till the bottom of the earth.

*Section (*Faṣl*)*

[380] The second interpretation is given by Shaykh Abū 'Alī Sīnā [i.e. Avicenna][1] and explained by [Naṣīr al-Dīn Ṭūsī],[2] his commentator on his *Ishārāt,* the explicator of his *tanbīhāt,*[3] may their innermost consciousness be sanctified by a way-station, about the degrees of rational soul in its ascension to the Lordly world.

The 'niche' (stands) for the material intellect [of man], which is tenebrous in essence but capable of receiving intellectual lights in varying degrees of proximity and distance according to its preparedness. The 'glass' is the intellect *in habitus* because it is transparent in itself [like the glass] and very receptive to the [intellectual] light like 'a radiant star' [receptive to the physical light]. The 'olive tree' is the cogitative and reflective faculty (*al-*

---

1. Avicenna (Ibn Sina) (d. 428/1037) was foremost of the Muslim Peripatetic philosophers and one of the greatest medieval physicians. He has written many works in Arabic and some in Persian in both fields. His medical work *al-Canon* was an important treatise on medicine both in East and West until the end of the eighteenth century. His most important works in philosophy are *al-Shifā'* and *al-Ishārāt wa al-Tanbīhāt,* which were influential on later development of Islamic philosophy and the medieval Christian philosophy especially Thomism.
2. Naṣīr al-Dīn al-Ṭūsī (d. 672/1274) was a mathematician, astronomer, philosopher and Shī'a theologian. In philosophy his masterpiece is considered to be his commentary (*sharḥ*) on Ibn Sina's *al-Ishārāt wa al-Tanbīh,* in which he defends Avicenna against Fakhr al-Dīn al-Rāzī's criticism of some of Avicenna's philosophical views. This work in the academies of philosophy in Iran is considered to be the best treatise on Avicenna's philosophy and is still taught in Iran.
3. Cf. Naṣīr al-Dīn al-Tūsī, *Sharḥ al-ishārāt wa al-tanbīhāt,* vol. 2, pp. 353–357. Also M. E. Marmura's translation, 'Avicenna: On the Proof of Prophecies', in *Medieval Political Philosophy* edited by R. Lerner and M. Mahdi, pp. 116–117.

quwwat al-fikrīyya wa'l-fikr) because it is prepared and has become ready to receive [the intellectual] light by itself but after exerting a great deal of movement and effort. It is 'blessed' because it is able to organize [the data] to obtain the definitions of things and correct demonstrative proofs. This [cogitative faculty] 'is neither of the Orient nor of the Occident' because the cogitative power that attains universal meanings, mental notions and intelligible propositions is neither of the Occident [i.e.] of the material sensory existents nor of the Orient [i.e.], Active intellects subsisting by themselves. The 'oil' is the intuitive power [of the intellect] (*al-ḥads*) because it is quite near to [the essence of] the olive oil. 'Its oil well nigh would give light even if no fire' of the sacred power 'touched it'. That is because it would be intellect in actuality though nothing has brought it from potency to actuality. In 'light upon light' the latter is the acquired intellect. The intellectual forms are the 'light' and the soul receptive to them is 'other light'. The 'lamp' is the actual intellect, because it is luminous by itself without needing a light to acquire [its luminosity], and the 'fire' is the Active Intellect because the 'lamp' is kindled from it.

*Illuminative Unveiling (*Kashf Ishrāqī*)*

[381] Know that the saying of the Exalted 'neither of the Orient nor of the Occident', alluding to the 'olive tree', if taken in the intellectual sense would mean that it is outside the genus of places and inhering, as it is said, in the sphere that is neither hot nor cold, that is, it is outside the genus of these tactile qualities.

If it is taken in the corporeal sense alluding to the tree from which the oil is obtained and to the conic heart, then its meaning would be that it is something intermediary between the two [extremes], as is said of lukewarm water, which is neither hot nor cold. It is possible to predicate the 'Orient' to the next world and the 'Occident' to this world when by the 'tree' [which is neither of the Orient nor of the Occident] is intended [neither] the cogitative faculty nor the material faculty. The meaning of the negation of two extremes then will have two aspects: either the middle position between the two opposites or being outside the genus of the two.

It is possible to predicate the 'Orient' and the 'Occident' to the Necessary [Being] and contingent [beings respectively]. The essence of the Creator, the Glorified, is the 'place' of the rising of the lights of existents, and the world of contingent [beings] is the 'place' of the setting of those lights; in it there is the setting of the stars of the realities of [the Divine] Names. Then it would necessarily [follow] that by the 'niche' is intended the universal nature pervading differently in the bodies; and the 'glass' is the Universal Soul transparent in its essence, receptive to the Intellectual light in complete receptivity; the 'olive tree' is the divine power branched off in different ways to bring into existence the variegated realities according to the exigency of the beautiful Divine Names and the Forms of knowledge of God, which precede their different loci of manifestation and their differentiated existents. The Divine Power being something relative and inherent in the essence of the Divine Unity 'is neither of the Orient nor of the Occident' according to the meaning already mentioned. The 'oil' is the Will of God necessary for giving luminosity and illumination. It is without any need to join anything that calls it, because the Exalted Existence is complete in His agency and existentiation, independent in force and power for the illumination of [382] the light of existence from Him to the universe 'even if no fire' of the final cause and the external occasion 'touched it'.

The 'lamp' is the Universal Intellect (*al-'aql al-kullī*), i.e. the world of intellects, for being constantly shining in its essence, being sanctified from the adulteration of potency and preparedness and being enlightened by the light emanating from the Bounteous Reality on its essence at its witnessing the reality, may He be Glorified, and the illumination of the light of God on it. So it is 'light upon light God guides to His light whom He will' from among His servants. That is [to say] the totality of all the existents that are contingent essences are guided by the light of Existence [leading them] to their utmost essential goal through the First noetic originated Light which is the goal [or end] of the contingent world.

*Subtle Point [Derived] from the Throne (*Nuktah 'Arshīyya*)*

It is possible that by the 'olive tree' is meant the totality of the world of corporeal bodies, for it is like the olive tree neither of the Orient nor of the Occident, because the totality constitutes the boundary for dimensions and what it encompasses, but as totality it is neither situated in a place nor in a dimension. Its 'oil' is the power of the Absolute Existence and the Nature pervading in it, for it [i.e. Nature] has the preparedness to accept the kindling and luminosity in degrees of lights in strength and weakness according to the difference of the oil of matters, the largeness or smallness of the wick from the corporeal spherical and elemental forms.

The 'niche' is the universal matter, i.e. the totality of [particular] matters. The 'lamp' is the Universal Soul, i.e. the totality of the world of souls connected to the bodies different in kindling and luminosity. Its 'light' is the Universal Intellect, i.e. the totality of the sacred intellects in their different degrees enlightened by the light of the Divine gnosis.

Just as the parts of lamp and their places are different in emitting light and luminosity, but in the centre of its connected parts is a particular place that is more intense in power and light than all, likewise among the sacred intellects [383] the First Intellect is the noblest of all the contingent [existents] in existence, more powerful than them in luminosity and illumination. It is the 'reality' of Muḥammad enlightened by the light of the Divine gnosis without any intermediary, so it is 'light upon light'. Besides him none can be illuminated by the light of the reality and none has His vision except through him. His, peace be upon him and upon his progeny, saying confirms that 'if Moses had been in my time he would have had to follow me.'

[The Fourth] Chapter

His saying:

> God guides to His light whom He wills.
> (*Yahdī Allāhu li-nūrihi man yashā'u*)

This light is the Muḥammadan light, the unveiler of the realities of things as they are. It is the goal that is ranked above the existence of the earlier prophets. Because it is the seed of Ṭubà of the contingent world, which the hand of the Most Merciful has planted; it is the fruit obtained from the tree of existence of the earth and the sky; it is the straight path to the presence of the Exalted Lord; it is the primordial nature (*fiṭrah*) of God on which He modelled and created mankind. So human beings (*khalq*), because of their primordial nature, are bound to accept the Muḥammadan light; the souls are naturally disposed to the obedience of the prophetic Law (*sharī'ah*) for arriving at the praiseworthy station if straying has not prevented them from travelling on the path and if temptation [has not led them away] from going towards the ultimate Goal.

[It is reported] in a tradition that the Messenger, peace be upon him and upon his progeny, [said]: 'The first thing which God created was my light',[1] and also from him: 'Indeed, God created Adam in the image of the Most Merciful',[2] that is, He created the 'reality' of Muḥammad [384] in the image of [His] Name the 'Most Merciful' as He created Satan in the image of [His] Name the 'Avenger'. Also from him: 'Indeed God created my light from the light of His Might, and He created the light of Satan from the fire of His Might.'[3] This indicates that the spirit of seal of the prophets, peace be upon him and upon his progeny, is not from the genus of the rest of the spirits, as he, peace be upon him and upon his progeny, said: 'I am not like any one among you, for I stayed in the house with my Lord Who fed me and quenched my thirst.'[4]

So, O indigent, take heed and reflect that the lowest and most inferior of his states was staying in the house (with the Lord), taking food and drink from the Exalted Lord, so how could he be from the genus of the one who has not attained his eminent state such as [receiving] gnosis and [divine] reflection? The actions of the corporeal beings and the earthly souls, nay even the celestial souls, are further away in levels to ascend to the divine world.

The intellectual (or noetic) spiritual beings are different from each other in proximity to and distance from [the reality]. What reached God and became accepted by Him the Exalted without any intermediary was the Muḥammadan obediences and the Aḥmadī servanthood [owing to which] the lights of divine gnosis shone on his luminous essence without the mediation of anyone. So the obedience of other than him could not be like his obedience, it will be through the light of following him and through him only; so 'deem not the call of the Messenger among yourselves like the call of you to one another' [24:63].

1. *Aḥādīth-i Mathnawī*, no. 342.
2. *Ibid.*, no. 346 and no. 697.
3. *Tamhīdāt, op. cit.*, p. 267.
4. Cf. *supra*, note 76 in chapter three.

*Reminder (*Tadhkirah*)*

Sahl ibn 'Abdullāh al-Tustarī[1] and Shaybān al-Rā'ī said: 'We heard from Khiḍr, peace be upon him, who said: 'God created the light of Muḥammad, peace be upon him and upon his progeny, from His light; then He gave it a form, and placed [it] on His hand. That light remained in the hands of the Exalted for 100,000 years. He looked at it every day and night for 70,000 moments. Looking at every moment enveloped it in a new light and new magnanimity. Then He created all existents from it.''[2]

In [this report] there is an allusion to the emanation of creations, their forms and traces at every moment in [385] innumerable number through the light of the most noble contingency, the Muḥammadan aspect, the 'most holy emanation', which is the seed of existents, their prior essential efficient cause, the fruit of the tree of the contingent [existents], its posterior final cause. It is the first and the last because it is the kernel of the kernels, and the seal of the Book for the existence.

*Similitude of the Throne (*Tamthīl 'Arshī*)*

O gnostic! Reflect on the wisdom of the Creator the Originator, on the Being of the Giver of benefit, the Impregnable, the Exalted, how He began by the Intellect and ended by the intelligent. Between the two there are various interconnecting degrees in hierarchy.

The first Intellect is the seed of the intelligent ones and the source (or principle) of the noble ones. Apart from it the Intellects preceding the bodies are its stems; the Universal Soul is its branches; the celestial bodies are its stalks and twigs; the earthly souls are its flowers; the human souls are its precious fruits; the acquired

1. Sahl ibn 'Abdūllah al-Tustarī (d. 283/896) was an early Ṣūfī from Tustar, now known as Shūshtar in Iran.
2. *Tamhīdāt, op. cit.*, pp. 267–268.

intellects are the kernels of its seeds and its lights; the Muḥammadan spirit is the quintessence of its kernel, its oil and the luminosity of its lamp.

So know what has been mentioned; actualize what has been recited to you; contemplate on it and do not take it as a poetical allegory but as the realization of the '*sirr*', and recite His saying: 'His Command governs the affairs from heaven to Earth' [32:5]. Follow His Command in what He says: 'Be the worshippers of the Lord' [3:79]. If that is not possible by yourself then benefit from the others [in this matter], for a believer is the mirror of the believer.

A certain gnostic said in his supplication: 'O my God, what is the wisdom in my creation?' In response God inspired him by His saying: 'Indeed the wisdom in thy creation is My vision in the mirror of thy spirit, and My love in thy heart.'[1] How great is the degree of a servant who has faith, and what a lofty [station he has] when the plane of his heart becomes a mirror for the Face of the reality, so whenever He desires He self-manifests His self for His self by looking at the heart of the believer!

[386] It is recorded in a report that 'God has three hundred and sixty looks in a day and night at the heart of the believer'. This is supported by his saying, peace be upon him and upon his progeny: 'Indeed God does not look at your forms and your deeds, but He looks at your hearts and your intentions',[2] and His saying: 'Does he not know that God sees?' [96:14].

It is recorded in a sacred tradition (*al-ḥadīth al-qudsī*) that He said: 'I was a hidden treasure ... then I created the creatures and thereby made Myself known to them.'[3]

---

1. *Ibid.*, p. 272.
2. *Aḥādīth-i Mathnawī*, no. 150.
3. *Ibid.*, no. 70.

This fruit for the creation and existentiation – which is the gnosis (*ma'rifah*) of God – is realized in a servant having faith, i.e. a gnostic, as He says: 'I created the jinn and humankind only that they serve Me' [51:56], i.e. they know [Him]. It has been established that he who is a gnostic is the ultimate goal of the existentiation of the spheres, the elements and composite beings according to His saying in a sacred tradition: 'If not for you I would not have created the spheres.'[1] This is supported by the saying of the Sublime: 'The sights perceive Him not, but He perceives the sights' [6:103], and His saying: 'Are they still in doubt concerning the meeting with their Lord? Does He not encompass all things?' [41:54].

*Admonition and Allusion (*Tanbīh wa Ishārah*)*

It is for you to understand from these mysteries that the perception of the essence of the Exalted Reality by the unprecedented knowledge is possible only in the mirror of the heart of a faithful who is pious; and it is because of that He made the world, created the generated beings and originated the order [of the universe], as He says: 'We shall show them Our signs on the horizons and in themselves, till it is clear to them that it is the truth. Suffices it not as to thy Lord, that He is Witness over all things?' [41:53]; [387] and His saying: 'And in yourselves, do you not see?' [51:21].

Also, besides what we have mentioned, what stands out is his saying, peace be upon him and upon his progeny, that 'He who has seen me has indeed seen the reality',[2] and His saying 'So he who obeys the Messenger has obeyed God' [4:80]. There is a tradition from him, peace be upon him and upon his progeny, 'Oh! How I yearn to meet my brothers who [come] after me'; and what Kumayl ibn Ziyād has narrated from the Commander of the Faithful ['Alī ibn Abī Ṭālib]

1. *Ibid.*, no. 546.
2. *Ibid.*, no. 163.

similar to this in a long discourse,[1] and the saying of the Prophet, peace be upon him and upon his progeny, that 'My Lord taught me courtesy, so how beautiful has been His teaching me courtesy'[2] allude to that. Also, in His saying 'and I blew into him My spirit' [15:29] there is a great admonition in it; and also in His saying 'but man carried it' [33:72].

It is given in the symbolic [writings of] some companion of the heart concerning the [esoteric] exegesis of His saying 'I was a hidden treasure ...', that 'servitude without lordship is deficiency and evanescence, and lordship without servitude is impossible.'[3]

Some of the allusions for this purpose [are given] in His sayings: 'And [Allah] bound them to the word of piety (*al-taqwā*), and well were they entitled to it and worthy of it' [48:26]; and 'God has bought from the believers their souls and their possessions because the Garden will be theirs' [9:111]. And the subtle supportive [indications] to this claim in His sayings that '[Man] has indeed been unjust and ignorant' [33:72]; and 'Surely man is in a state of loss, save those who believe and do righteous deeds' [103:2–3]. From all this [information] it is learned that what is appropriate for the reality and His vision is the gnosis of the reality, and not the man nor the others from the existents of the contingent world, for 'what has the dust to do with the Lord of the lords'.[4]

Nearer to this is what some realized from the saying of one of the sages: 'He who says that the Necessary (Being) [388] is existent, and he who makes this proposition from the contingent world is not one of the minds. Rather, it is one of the aspects of the demonstration.' So reflect on His saying: 'By the star when it falls,

1. Cf. *Nahj al-Balāghah* with commentary of Muḥammad 'Abduh, part 4, p. 38, and its translation in *Living and Dying with Grace: Counsels of Ḥadrat 'Alī* by T. Cleary, p. 83. The contents of *Nahj al-Balāghah* are attributed to the first Shī'ite Imam, 'Ali ibn Abī Ṭālib (d. 41/661).
2. *Tamhīdāt*, pp. 174, 274.
3. *Ibid.*, p. 275.
4. Arabic proverb.

your comrade is not astray, nor deceived, nor does he speak out of caprice. This is naught save a revelation that is revealed, which one of the mighty Powers has taught him' [53:1–5]; and 'then He revealed to His servant that which He revealed. His heart lied not of what it saw' [53:10–11].[1]

*Unveiling of the Spiritual State for the Verification of Discourse (*Kashf Ḥāl li-Taḥqīq Maqāl*)*

O my friend, reflect on the difference between the [spiritual] level of Moses, peace be upon him, and the [spiritual] level of our master and our Prophet, peace be upon him and upon his progeny. Moses fell down swooning unconscious at beholding the [divine] self-manifestation at the mount [Sinai, as He says]: 'And when his Lord manifested Himself to the mountain He made it come crashing down. And Moses fell down swooning' [7:143]. Then he turned [to Him] and repented for seeking what was not in his capacity and was untimely. But the Prophet, peace be upon him and upon his progeny, reports about himself that, on the night of the ascension, God put His hand between his shoulders, and he felt the coldness of His fingertips between his breasts.[2]

The above tradition gives a clear indication of the love of Him the Exalted for His lover [i.e. Muḥammad]. If you are in doubt about what we have mentioned then I add to it what I have heard from a tradition [which states]: 'I stayed in the house with my Lord',[3] and another tradition: 'He who has seen me [has indeed seen the

---

1. According to the traditional source this Qur'ānic verse is in the context of Prophet Muḥammad's direct experience of the reality during his nocturnal ascent. Ṣadrā in his major metaphysical works interprets 'one of the mighty Powers' by different names such as Gabriel, Active Intellect, Father and Holy Spirit. By 'heart' he means the rational soul.
2. *Tamhīdāt*, p. 277.
3. Cf. note 76 in chapter three.

reality]."[1] Now all that we have transmitted in this context is to make clear to you the truth of the words of his [Prophet Muḥammad's] brother [i.e.] his cousin ['Alī ibn Abī Ṭālib], his sharer in his affliction and sorrow, his 'associate in his portion and share',[2] the 'inheritor of his basin',[3] and the 'gate to the city of his knowledge',[4] when he, peace of God be upon both and their progeny, said: 'My heart saw my Lord',[5] and also: 'I did not look at a thing save I saw God in it.'[6] This is a similitude of His saying: 'Have you not seen how thy Lord has spread the shadow?' [25:45].

*Allusion (*Ishārah*)*

[389] Know O [my] beloved! Only the light knows the worth of the light, nay each degree from it knows only what occurs in the genus of that degree. The sensible light perceives the sensible light; the light of the soul perceives the light of the soul; and the light of the intellect perceives the light of the intellect. Only the light of the sight can perceive the light of the stars, and only the lights of the

---

1. *Aḥādīth-i Mathnawī*, no. 163.
2. This implies that 'Alī ibn Abī Ṭālib inherited a share in *walāyah* from the Prophet, which, according to Shī'ite theology, is the esoteric mission of the Friends of God, i.e. the twelve Imams including 'Alī, to initiate their followers into the mysteries of the Qur'ān. H. Corbin has written extensively on this Shī'ite doctrine. Cf. his *En Islam iranien*, vol. 1, chap. 2, pp. 39–43.
3. The reference is to a tradition attributed to the Prophet, which is known in Shī'ite traditional sources as '*ḥadīth thaqalayn*' (tradition pertaining to 'two weighty things'). It is considered by Shī'ite scholars to be one of the most strongly established traditions in connection with the appointment of 'Alī ibn Abī Ṭālib as his successor to the leadership (*imamate*) of the Muslim community and after him his male progeny through his wife Fāṭimah to be the Imams of the Muslim community. The tradition is as follows. 'The Prophet said: I leave two weighty things among you, the Book of God and the People of My House. These two will never be separated from each other until they encounter me at the Basin (of Kawthar in Paradise).' Cf. *Tafsīr al-Qummī*, by Abū'l- Ḥasan Ibrāhim al-Qummī (d. circa 307/919–20), vol. 1, p. 30.
4. The reference is to the tradition of the Prophet in connection with his relation to 'Alī ibn Abī Ṭālib. It is as follows: 'I am the city of knowledge and 'Alī is its gate.' Cf. *Aḥādīth-i Mathnawi*, no. 90.
5. *Tamhīdāt, op. cit.*, pp. 12, 202, etc.
6. *Ibid.*, pp. 56, 280.

senses can perceive the lights of the sensibles with a condition that they are annihilated from the qualities particular to them. [For instance] the power of touch is from the genus of four qualities, which are the primary qualities of touch save that it is balanced and a mean among them. You have learned that anything that is a mean between the two extremes is in the position of being bereft of the two and that is why it can receive them, perceive them and sense them. The moisture of the saliva, for instance, which is released from the matter of tongue, has no taste in itself. But its nature is that it is qualified by the quality of [food and drink] which possess flavour, and the faculty of taste perceives it whose relation to all foods is equal despite being situated in the genus of the qualities of taste. Accordingly you may infer the same about the rest of the senses and organs of perception, etc., up to the world of intellect and the intelligible and beyond it, as the proverb goes: 'No one can carry the gifts of the sovereigns save the beasts of the sovereigns.'

A certain Shaykh was asked: 'What is the proof of God?' He replied: 'His proof is that He is God.'[1] The most learned scholar Fakhr al-Dīn Rāzī[2] asked the gnostic Shaykh Najm al-Dīn[3]: 'By what did you know thy Lord?' He answered: 'By the [inspirational] inrushes irrupting in the hearts which make the souls incapable of falsifying them.'

So beyond reason there is knowledge, which is subtler than what could be perceived by even the utmost limits of the sound reasons.

---

1. *Ibid.*, p. 283.
2. Fakhr al-Dīn al-Rāzī (d. 606/1209), originally from the ancient city of Rayy, died in Herat in present-day Afghanistan. He was an Ash'arite Kalām theologian and well versed in the philosophical works of al-Fārābī and Avicenna. Some of his major works are *Mabāḥith al-mashriqīyya* and *Tafsīr al-kabīr,* which is his commentary on the Qur'ān in thirty-two volumes.
3. Najm Dāyāh Rāzī (d. 654/1256) was a prolific writer of Ṣūfī works and an important master in the Kubrawīyah Ṣūfī order of Central Asia. His famous work is *Mirsād al-Ibād* which is a handbook of Kubrawī Ṣūfī teaching. It has been translated into English by Hamid Algar.

One of the spiritually realized ones said: 'The proof of the gnosis of God for the beginner [on the spiritual wayfaring] is his love and desire [for Him], for the two awaken (*yunba'athān*) from the gnosis though little and weak [in the beginning]. Their relation to the perfect [divine] witnessing is like the relationship of seed to fruit. Thus the mover of the hearts towards the Exalted Reality is His essence, so 'I cannot enumerate the praise of Thee [390] as Thou hast praised thyself'.

A certain Shaykh said: 'Indeed God the Exalted revealed to the Messenger of God on the night of (his) Ascension that O Muḥammad, you were at all moments in the state of seeing and hearing; I am God, the Hearer and Seer, and you are the receiver and the object of [my] seeing'.[1] 'Then He revealed to His servant that which He revealed' [53:10].

Section (Faṣl)

Concerning the explanation of the essence (or reality, *māhīyya*) of the Perfect Man – the microcosm – the locus of manifestation of the Name 'Allah' – the all-comprehensive [Name] for the loci of manifestation of all the divine Names

He [i.e. the Perfect Man] is the vicegerent of God on His earth and the symbol of the light of God in His heaven; he is the one who is [the image of] the Deity (*ilāh*) in heaven and of the Deity on earth. He the Glorified said: 'And He taught Adam all the names, then showed them to the angels, saying: Inform Me of the names of these, if you are truthful. They said: Glory be to Thee! We have no knowledge save that which Thou hast taught us. Surely Thou, only Thou, art the Knower, the Wise' [2:31–32].

> It is not impossible for God that He brings together the world in one [being].

1. *Tamhīdāt, op. cit.*, p. 277.

Know that every existent from the differentiated existents that are the parts of this world is the locus of manifestation of a particular Name from the Names of God the Exalted. As in the parts of this world there are genera, species, individuals, substances and accidents [such as] quantity, quality, when, where, position, relation, passivity, activity, possession. Likewise, in the divine Names there are Names that are similar to genus, to species, substance, accident, quantity, quality, etc. Also in the Perfect Man – the all-comprehensive locus of [divine] manifestation – is found all that exists in the world of Names, and in the horizontal loci of manifestation.

As the Names, all of them, are synthesized with regard to their differentiated meanings in the Name 'Allah', likewise the realities of their loci of manifestation, which are the parts of the horizontal macrocosm, [391] are combined in the locus of manifestation of the Name Allah, and that [locus] is the Perfect Man, the microcosm, in some way, and macrocosm, nay higher [than that], in another way. This is with regard to his encompassing all the existents, their principles, their causes, their forms and their goals by the knowledge emanated (lit. awakened) from the mine of the knowledge of God. As the Commander of the Faithful ['Alī ibn Abī Ṭālib], the Imam of the gnostics, the head of the people of unification (*al-muwaḥḥīdūn*), peace be upon him, said:

> You are the manifest book by whose signs what is hidden in it manifests,
> You claim that you are a small body, but in thee is enveloped the macrocosm.

Therefore we say concerning the explanation of what we mentioned in the introductions, and the clarification of what we derive from the narratives:

Every contingent is a locus of manifestation of a particular Name [of God]. So it entails that there is a stable relation between the giver of emanation and the receiver of emanation. The plurality of perfections and the multiplicity of forms of objects of knowledge indicate the realization of those universal meanings and goodness in their (secondary) reasons and causes in a higher and more complete way without the necessity of multiplicity and embodiment in their primary cause, as has been established in Transcendent Theosophy (*al-Ḥikmat al-muta'ālīyah*).

The intention behind each one of the Names of God is none but His essence. [Each Name] is derived along with a particular Attribute from His Attributes of perfection, negation or relation such as Living, Powerful, All-Holy. His Essence is qualified by all the perfect, beautiful Attributes and transcends all imperfections, shortcomings and flaws, and He has a self-subsisting relation to everything besides Him.

When considering their attribution to Him as such, the first in succession to emerge are the beautiful, benevolent and positive Names; when considering them to be sanctifying Him from what He is not; the second in succession to emerge are the majestic, dominant and negative (*salbīyya*) Names; when considering the illumination of His light, His witnessing and emanating the munificence of His Existence on the existents, it is the emergence of the relative connective [Names]. Since it is necessary to realize the relation between the giver of emanation and [392] the receiver (or the object) of emanation, so anyone whose relation [to the agent of emanation] is more intensive is nearer (to it) in the degree of being-caused.

Every real agent [i.e. the efficient cause] for the contingents is also the final cause as it has been proved in its [appropriate] place. So it entails that the emanation from it in the chain according to proximity and distance in descent ascends to it in another chain according to proximity and distance in ascent.

This matter is evident according to complete induction concerning all contingents that they have generated from the natural agent [or the efficient cause] for the sake of the essential goal. It has detailed explanation which needs a thorough examination of the discourses on 'cause and caused', the rules of the final cause whose end is the realization of efficient cause in a perfect way. It does not make any difference if the final cause is later in existence than the efficient cause, as in [those existences] that are generated, or the two are one essence, as in [those existences] that are beyond generation.

If this is established then [know that] the noblest existent issued from Him the Exalted in the chain of origin is the First Intellect, the noble contingent being. After the noble the [less] noble to the most low, then from the most low (contingent) to the degree of Existence ends at the corporeal bodies. These are the matters of divine arts like a piece of wood for the carpenter. Then from it [i.e. the corporeal body] begins the gradual perfection by the forms and the ascent to the ultimate perfection. It is conceived as form after form and mode after mode like the forms and shapes in succession on the wood that the carpenter's art leaves on it by the act of shaping and marking. So the forms follow each other on the matters according to the gradual perfection of preparedness from the ignoble to the noble, then from the noble (form) free from defect and weakness and separated from obscurity and deficiency to the acquired intellect connected to the Active Intellect. It is the highest degree of existence in the world of contingents, because it includes the forms of all existents – intelligible and sensible – with regard to its essence, its soul and its body to which we will allude [soon].

[393] By the acquired intellect, the existence returns to the Origin from which it began, and reaches the height of perfection after falling from it. [As He the Exalted said:] 'As We originated the first creation, so shall We bring it back' [21:104].

Just as the First Intellect includes all that issues from it – from goodness, existences, forms and shapes according to the primordial nature – so is the intellect situated parallel to it, nay it is identical to it in some respect, as is the view of those deeply rooted in the spiritual discipline and demonstration and of those who are assiduous in faith and disengagement [from the appetites], that it contains everything with respect to attainment and acquisition for the second existential nature that corresponds to the primordial nature pertaining to decreed knowledge.

This is the intention of the saying of the eminent philosopher Aristotle, that 'he who desires philosophy then let him create the second nature for his self'. Philosophy according to him [means] to resemble God according to human capacity. This is actualized by attaining the Active Intellect.

*Inspirational Subtle Point (*Daqīqah Ilhāmīyya*)*

Here there is another subtle point, which the majority of the eminent scholars have not been able perceive nor to speak of other than they who are the prisoners of estimation and fantasy. [That point is], though the Active Intellect is the agent antecedent to contingent [beings], it is precisely the fruit obtained from their existences that are ordered hierarchically in gradual perfection and ascent towards perfection. Although it is true and there is no doubt about it for this indigent, broken in heart, distressed in state, yet it is one of the strange things.

*Enlightening Reminder (*Inārah Tadhakkurīyya*)*

The Names of God the Exalted are inclusive of all the rational and concrete (*al-'aynīyya*) meanings, all the substantial and accidental realities. If you observe the realities of things [394] you will find that some are followed and encompass the accidents, and some follow. We call those that are followed 'substances' and those that follow 'accidents'. Know that the meaning of substantiality from the point of the association of substances in it, its unity in its very integrity, is the locus of manifestation of the divine Essence with regard to its self-subsistence and its realization by itself. The accidents are associated with each other in the accidental meaning occurring to them though they are different from each other. They are the loci of manifestation for the divine Attributes which are subject to the (divine) Essence. Although in being Attributes, they are subject to the divine Essence, they are associated with each other, whereas the Being is the unity of Essence and Attributes.

Further, just as the reality of substances is always concealed by the accidents, likewise the divine Essence is veiled from the others by Names and Attributes. Just as when a substance joins with one of the attributes it becomes a particular substance, a manifestation for a particular name, so is the divine Essence when considered with a particular Attribute, a particular Name from the universal and particular Names.

Just as from the particular qualities of the substances, such as differentia, etc., some are general and some are particular, like proximate and distant differentia and their concomitants, so that by their inclusion or annexation the substance becomes a particular genus or species, likewise among the divine Attributes there are those that are general and more encompassing, and there are those that are particular and less encompassing. So the Name obtained from the annexation of what is more general corresponds to genus, [and] the Name obtained from the annexation of what is more particular would correspond to species. The example of [the Name] which corresponds to genus is All-Knowing, and to species All-Hearing and All-Seeing.

Just as by the unification of simple substances other composite substances come into existence, likewise by the unification of universal [divine] Names other Names come into existence.

Also a substance may be a simple species externally, composite in the mind with regard to mental analysis, such as, intellect, soul and the other than [these] two; and it may be externally composite from the parts of [395] spiritual existences such as matter and form; or the contrary parts of natures such as the composites of mineral, plant and animal. Likewise, in the different kinds of [divine] Names there are those that are simple and objective, possessing differentiated limit such as 'Living'. Its notion is derived from [such Names as] the 'Perceiver', 'Active'; and there are those that are composed, like the 'Living, Self-Subsisting'.

Just as the totality of substances and the species is limited, so is the totality of the [divine] Names. Just as individual substances are unlimited, likewise the subdivisions of the [divine] Names are unlimited. Just as all associate in one existential nature, because the contingent existence is one reality which is named the 'breath of Mercifulness', the 'intelligible Matter' [which is] the substratum for the intelligible and sensible forms and their realities, likewise one divine Essence is inclusive of the totality of [divine] Names, and synthesizes all the Names with their different meanings.

Further, the divine epiphanies manifesting the multiple qualities according to the rule 'each day He is upon some task' [55:29] are unlimited, and despite the limitation of their rules they occur repeatedly [owing to which] the accidents become multiple; they are unlimited although the principal ones are limited. Just as the principal accidents are limited to nine categories, likewise in the principal universal [divine] Attributes meanings are found which correspond to those categories.

Further, everything in existence is a proof and a sign of what is in the invisible. [The divine Name] 'Self-Subsisting' corresponds to substance, and the 'Sacred' to single species from it. The 'Giver of form' [corresponds] to substantial forms; the 'First and the Last' to the category 'when'; the 'Uplifter and Diminisher' correspond to the category 'where'; the 'Prior and Posterior' to the category 'place'; the 'Reckoner' to 'disjunctive quantity; the 'Great, the Powerful, the Expansive' to 'conjunctive quantity'; the 'Hearer and the Seer' to 'psychic quality', the 'Most Lofty' to 'the relation'; the 'King of kings' to the 'position'; the 'Originator' to the 'act'; [396] the 'Receiver of penitence' to the 'passive'.

When investigated deeply, it appears that each meaning existent in the visible (or manifest) world is a shadow indicating what is in the invisible world of Names. From there [it descends] to the invisible world of the divine Decree, I mean the Intellectual Pen, then to the world of psychic Allotment, I mean the Tablet of the decreed sciences called 'the essence of the Book' (*umm al-kitāb*), then to the world of heavenly Tablets and their imaginative imprinted souls called 'the book which blots out and establishes' and 'two emerald covers' as His saying [indicates]: 'God obliterates what He wills, and establishes [what He wills], and with Him is the essence of the Book' [13:39].

*Guidance (*Hidāyah*)*

It has been made clear to you and you must have comprehended from what has been presented to you that all these worlds are the Books and Scriptures of the All Merciful, which are encompassed by the forms of realities and meanings and which include numbers and lines indicating the glorifying praises and lordly laudation, which when a gnostic reader recites by his faculty of cogitation, by the purity of his '*sirr*', by his nature free from the turbidity of attachments [to appetites], by the purity of his mind and by his eye stripped of attachments to these 'coverings', then he comes to know what is in them. If he reflects on their meanings, then from some [meanings] he ascends to some [other] until he arrives at their Originator, at their Recorder, their Dictator, their Agent of Order [and he cannot help] saying: 'Glory be to Him who carried His servant by night from the Inviolable Mosque to the Further Mosque the precincts of which We have blessed, that We might show him of Our signs. He, only He is the Hearer, the Seer' [17:1].

*Comprehensive Logos (*Kalimah Jāmi'ah*)*

The Perfect Man is a comprehensive book of the signs of His Lord the All Holy; a rolled-up scroll in which are the realities of intellects and souls; a perfect 'word' full of various sciences and [their] branches; a copy written from the symbol of 'Be and it becomes'. Nay, he is a command recorded in the '*kāf* and *nūn*' [i.e. *kun*, meaning the divine Command 'be'], because he is the epiphany of the greatest [divine] name 'Allāh' [397], which encompasses all [divine] Names.

With regard to his spirit and intellect he is the Sacred Pen called 'the essence of the Book' because he contains the great universal intellectual truths in the sacred intellectual way. With regard to his real heart, I mean his rational soul, he is 'the Book of the Guarded Tablet', because his imprints are forever guarded by the protection of the Pen of the Scribe of these writings – the active [agent] for the differentiated intelligibles in the tablet of his heart. With regard to his animal soul conceiving the imaginative forms he is 'a book that blots and establishes'. With regard to his corporeal nature subsisting by the fine vapour resembling the matter of heaven receptive to the lights of the senses and luminescence, he is 'a corporeal record' and 'a scroll constituted of matter'.

The purpose of bringing him to existence and his generation is only for the exercise and reckoning, like a plank and dust are for the benefit of the exercise of the infant soul before it reaches the station of a man, like the tablets of children because what is written in it could be rubbed off and withdrawn quickly, being from the genus of the 'book of licentiousness', which is thrown in the fire. In addition to it are the four books of the principles; all of them are the pure elevated scriptures purified by the hands of the Emissaries, noble and upright, which will remain till the Day of Religion [i.e. the Day of Resurrection]; none can touch them but those purified from the corporeal veils, because they are in '*Illīyyūn*, 'and what conveys unto you what *'Illīyyūn* is! A written book witnessed by those drawn near [unto their Lord]' [83:19–21].

This last book is parallel to the heavenly form, its pages will be set on fire by the fire of Nature, just as the scroll of the circular [motions] of the heavens will be rolled up on the Day of Resurrection as the Exalted said: 'On the Day when We shall roll up heaven as a scroll is rolled for writings' [21:104]. But it will be according to the requisite of 'as We originated the first creation, so shall We bring it back' [21:104]. The likeness of him will return on the Day of Resurrection and Gathering. This is the body of the next world[1] awakened from the effaced, this worldly [or elemental] body which is buried after death, but its book remains till the Day of Resurrection. It is the book to which is referred in His saying: 'And every man's acts [lit. bird, *ṭā'ir*] have We fastened to his neck; and We shall bring forth for him, on the Day of Resurrection, a book which he shall find wide open. [And it will be said to him]: Recite thy book! Sufficient is your own self today as to make out your account' [17:13–14].

[398] This book will be divided into the book of the wicked who will be cast into the Fire and the book of the pious who will come through safe on the Day of Resurrection, as He says: 'Is he who is cast into the Fire better, or he who comes safe through on the Day of Resurrection?' [41:40] These two [verses] indicate the two [books] in His saying 'Surely the book of the vile is in the *Sijjīn*' [83:7] and His saying 'And verily the book of the righteous is in *'Illīyyūn*' [83:18].

1. On the body of resurrection, cf. our article on 'Reincarnation or Resurrection of the Soul? Mullā Ṣadrā's Philosophical Solution to the Dilemma', in *Transcendent Philosophy*, vol. 3:2, pp. 115–130.

*[Perfect Man] is Comprehensive Light and Comprehensive Locus of Divine Epiphany (*Nūr Jamʿī wa Maẓhar Jāmʿi Ilāhī*)*

It has already been mentioned that Perfect Man is the comprehensive Logos [of the signs of God], and the Model containing what is in the divine Books, all of which are lights written by the Hand of the All Merciful, printed on the scriptures of the generated beings, hidden from the eyes of the blind. In just this way does the Great Spirit brings together all that is in the macrocosm being the principle of all, the form of all, the goal of all, the seed of intellects and souls, the fruit of the tree of spheres and what is in them from the intelligible and sensible lights.

Now we would like to explain to you the degrees of the human world and its names. The human spirit – the last lordly Intellect [i.e. the Active Intellect] – is on the level of proximity to God in the world of Return and Ascent. It is the similitude of the Great Spirit and the first Qur'ānic Intellect in the world of Origin and Descent [respectively]. Its power on the Day of Resurrection and the Day of Action is like the power of the Great Spirit on the Day of pre-eternity because of its inclusiveness of both in all the degrees of being.

Rather the First Intellect and the final spirit – and it is the reality of Muḥammad – are one essence manifested twice, once after the creation to complete the creatures, and once before [or in front of] the Exalted Reality, for their intercession, as he, peace be upon him and upon his progeny, says: 'The first thing which God created was my light',[1] and his saying [399] 'The first creation which God created was the Intellect. He said to it: Come forward. It came forward. Then He said to it: Go backward. It went backward. He said: By my might and majesty! I have not created a creation mightier than thee; by thee I will give, by thee I will take back; by thee I will reward, by

1. *Aḥādith-i Mathnawī*, no. 343.

thee I will punish."[1] This [tradition] has been narrated by the traditionist Shaykh Muḥammad bin Ya'qūb al-Kulaynī[2] at the beginning of the chapter on 'Intellect' in his the Book *al-Kāfī*. This is a tradition which is sound according to the general consensus [of the Traditionsts].

Just as the Great Spirit is inclusive of all contingents in knowledge and externally, so is this Perfect Man the vicegerent (*khalīfah*) of God in the heavens and the earth.

As for the encompassing of the Great Spirit in knowledge it is as follows: It has already been discussed that it is the Pen of the First Reality; it is the donor of Forms to the realities in such a way that it is sanctified from multiplicity and differentiation. It is the scribe of the divine writings of mysteries on the tablets of allotments, because the Preserved Tablet and its contents are the writings and inscriptions proceeding from it and are present with it. It reads whatever is in it like the intellect reading the thoughts produced from it which are inscribed on the tablet of the soul, then on the tablet of the imagination and then on the senses.

So is the case with the rest of the universal organs of comprehension, the organs of perception of the spheres, the spirits of decree which contain the imaginal writings, the particular imaginative souls obtained in the imprinted heavenly souls. Likewise are the earthly forms inscribed on the tablets of matter. All of them issue from it by the permission of its Lord and are present with it. It witnesses them by the Light of its Lord by which the heavens and the earth are illuminated.

---

1. Cf. *Uṣūl al-Kāfī*, *op. cit.*, vol. 1, p. 10, no. 1.
2. Muḥammad ibn Ya'qūb al-Kulaynī (d. 329/940) came from a village near Rayy, now called Kulayn, in Iran. He lived in Baghdad and died there. His work *Uṣūl al-Kāfī* in several volumes is a collection of the Traditions of the Prophet and the Shī'ite Imams. It is the earliest authoritative source for Shī'ite jurisprudence, theology, and spiritual sciences.

Also, each one of its intellectual and psychic substances, the heavenly and sensory forms, the solar and lunar lights are the seeing eyes, the radiant organs of perceptions and polished mirrors by which things are perceived, and whatever is in the realm of earth and heaven is obtained.

As for its encompassing whatever is external, it is as follows. The essence of the Great Spirit is the Form of all [existents]. Also it is its efficient and final [cause]. The form in every composed reality and specific quiddity is the completion of that quiddity. Do you not see that [400] a bed is a bed thanks to its particular form and not because of the wooden obscure matter; an animal is an animal by its soul and senses and not by its body and corporeality? Likewise the efficient cause is the completion of the reality of the caused, because the caused emerges in its existence from the cause and is effused by it, like the rays from the sun, the heat from the fire, the moistness from the ocean, as is explained by the theosophists (*al-ilāhiyyūn*) in their divine sciences. As for the final cause, it is the completion of the efficient cause being the efficient and its perfection.[1]

As for the intellectual spirit of the perfect man encompassing all contingent [existents] that is because it is the 'clear book' which is inclusive of the samples of the worlds, their portions, their parts and units. This is before its connecting to the higher plenum and the Great Spirit. But at its connection there is no difference between it and the Pen of the First the Reality in its encompassing all.

*Divine Wisdom in Adamic Logos (*Ḥikmat Ilāhīyya fī Kalīmah Ādamīyya*)*

Among the wonders of the art of God and the novelties of His creation one is the creation of Man whom God has created as a

1. On the issue of efficient cause according to Ṣadrā, cf. our article on 'Mullā Ṣadrā on the Theory of Causal Efficacy', forthcoming in the Proceedings of the 2nd International Conference on Mulla Sadra held at S.O.A.S. London in 2001.

cosmos resembling the divine world. God has created him as a creation that integrates all that is in the rest of the worlds and creations. Nay, (He has created him) as an essence which is attributed with everything as is attributed to His essence such as His attributes of Beauty and Majesty, His Acts and Traces, His worlds, realms and creations, His Pen and Tablet, the Decree and Allotment, the angels and the spheres, the elements and the things composed [from the elements], heaven and hell, eternal happiness and possessor of the kingdom.

In sum, He created the Perfect Man as an image of Him the Exalted in essence, in attribute and action. The knowledge of this original creation, the subtle order and the knowledge of this meticulous wisdom and the mysteries hidden in it are a great secret of the knowledge of God. Rather, it is not possible to have knowledge of God except through knowledge of the Perfect Man. He is the great Gate of God and the firm grip, the strong rope by which one can climb to the higher world. He is the straight path to God the Omniscient and the Most Wise. He is the noble book [401] who has come from the Most Merciful, the Most Compassionate. Hence, it is necessary for everyone to have the knowledge of what is in this hidden book and to have the understanding of this treasured mystery.

This is the spiritual meaning of the necessity of the knowledge of the Prophet and the knowledge of the Imam, peace be upon them, for 'he who dies and has not known the Imam of his time has died the death of ignorance (*jāhilīyya*)'.[1] That is because the life of a man in the eternal mode of existence (*al-nash'at al-dā'imah*) is by the knowledge of the divine wisdom. In the Perfect Man all the wisdom is concealed. This is the essence of his [i.e. Prophet Muḥammad] saying: 'He who obeys me, obeys God', and his saying: 'He who knows his soul has known his Lord'.[2]

---

1. *Uṣūl al-Kāfī*, vol. 2, p. 208, no. 970.
2. *Aḥādith-i Mathnawī*, no. 529.

The intention behind [the above tradition] is the Prophet himself, which is ascertained by the saying of the Exalted: 'The Prophet is nearer to those who have faith than their own souls' [33:6]. That is because the prophetic reality perfects the souls of those who have faith by the light of its guidance and enlightens the intellects of men; it brings them out from potentiality to actuality, shines on them the knowledge of Light and gives them the existence [worthy] of the next world. So his essence is the cause of the realization of wisdom and faith in them and the actualization of their essence with regard to their subsisting existence and eternal stability. Now, the efficient cause of a thing is nearer to one's self because a thing by itself is a contingent [being], but by its cause and perfector it is a necessary [being]. Therefore, necessity and perfection are prior for a thing than contingency and deficiency.

So understand and reflect on what we have imparted to you about the meaning of the necessity of following the Prophet and the Imam [from his progeny]. Their beings are constituents for the essence of the believer *qua* believer. [This meaning] is unique at this moment which you will not find in other place than this. God is the Guide to the Abode of peace.

*Adamic Mirror which Contains the Signs of the Lord and the Lights of Mercy (*Mir'āt Ādamīyya fīhā āyāt Rabbānīyya wa anwār Raḥmānīyya*)*

Now, we will mention a sample of the book of divine wisdom and the quintessence of the Qur'ānic meanings [402] inscribed on this human copy, written by the wonderful divine writing. It is a clear book, a tablet inscribed by the inscriptions of the angels (*kirām al-kātibūn*, [Qur'ān, 82:11]), so it is a command for you to study this book given to you by the First Reality and to understand its aims. This above-mentioned writing is the 'guide' for you from the Forgiving Lord. It contains the investigation of divine issues and the explication of divine knowledge which can be derived from its writ and principles.

Thus we say: Know that the Universal Man according to the root of his essence by which he *qua* he is an existent, nay an existence subsistent by itself, is disengaged from time and space, transcends from being inhering [in something], and from the sensory indication and division. It is a light from the spiritual lights of God, a mystery from His intellectual [or noetic] mysteries, a face from the faces of His power, a sign from the signs of His wisdom, an eye from the divine Eyes, and a word from the Words of His knowledge and will. So these are his essential qualities and all of them are derived from the essential Divine Attributes and the great Majestic Attributes which have manifested in one of His servants.

With regard to his inherent and accidental states, he is knower, powerful, willer, hearer, seer, living, speaker, and other than these attributes. All these are like the Attributes of Majesty and Beauty of God for they are from the perfection of the existent *qua* existent. If they are found in the caused, then they must be found in the emanating cause in the most exalted and eminent way.

With regard to his acts, they are like the Acts of God, may majestic be His remembrance, just as the Acts of God the Exalted are divided into those that are in time, place, motions and matters called creations (*al-kā'ināt*), and those that are in places and matters and not in times and motions called inventions (*al-ikhtirā'iyyāt*), and those that transcend all those called originations (*al-ibdā'iyyāt*). Likewise, some of the acts produced from the substance of the essence of man resemble the (divine) origination. In these acts, he does not need any instrument (or sense faculty) and movement [of thought]. Such [acts are for instance] his perception of the true knowledge, [403] the true laws having certainty such as his faith in God, in His angels, in His scriptures, in His messengers, the return of the creations to their Creator. This [results] when his [material intellect] becomes an acquired intellect after repeated perceptions and multiple witnessing. Then it becomes independent of instruments [or sense faculties] and thought movements for calling to presence his treasures and benefiting from his intelligibles. Rather, whenever he directs (his attention) to an intelligible that intelligible becomes present before him as an idea before his non-material essence.

Some of (his acts) resemble the (divine) invention, such as the state when a form arises for him in (his) faculty of imagination. The intellectual benefits resemble (divine) origination and those of imagination resemble (divine) invention. Likewise is the case with his natural acts which occur from him in the body without reflection and meditation, such as the preservation of the temperament (*al-mizāj*), the attraction of food and the repulsion of (refuge from the body), the formation of his organs and their shape by the permission of God and by His speech, and assistance from God by the powers (lit. armies) which one cannot not see.

Some of his (acts) resemble (the act of) generation (by God). They are his external acts obtained by his will, purpose and movement such as, writing, eating, drinking and the rest of the bodily and psychic acts in which lie the welfare of his organs, his faculties and external senses in accordance with his living and his world. By the former he is led towards the betterment of his Return and by the latter he becomes prepared for the ultimate felicity.

As for his kingdom and world and his commands operating in his servants [i.e. his sense organs] and in his city, his microcosm, I mean his body and what is connected to it, it resembles the whole of macrocosm, i.e. the heavens and the earth and what is connected to these two. His command in the units of his world resembles the command of God in the units of the world. Just as God the Sublime's Acts from their issuing from the realm of their invisible Ground to the external loci of manifestation have four degrees, which are Providence, Decree, Tablet and external Allotment, as we have alluded to it, likewise the acts and their generations by God's vicegerent have four degrees.

[a] Whenever something issues from him its first aspect is in his hidden level of '*sirr*' which is the most invisible (aspect of his being); it is his non-differentiated intellect (*al-'aql al-ijmālī*), his Qur'ānic book. [b] Then it descends to the field of his inner heart – his rational soul – at his calling to presence by cogitation and his thinking by the help of some higher angels of God, for instance, the calling to presence the universal concepts and universal propositions [404], or major premises of syllogism. At the seeking of particular matter and its obtaining externally, and its calling to presence from the level of knowledge to the concrete level, there arises in him the determination to act. [c] Then by the help of angels governing the lower (realm) it descends to the treasury of his individualized particular imagination. It is the realm of particular conceptions and minor premises of syllogism, which when connected to the major premises provide him with a particular view, which is a firm determination for the act. [d] Then he moves his parts (of the body) at will for their expression through the help of some armies of motion of God, and that intended act manifests according to the will that follows the concept and cogitation.

The first act corresponds to the (divine) Providence and the non-differentiated Decree (*al-qaḍā' al-ijmālī*). Its substrate is the intellectual spirit, which corresponds to the Pen. The second form corresponds to the inscription on the Preserved Tablet. The third one corresponds to the form of heaven, for the spirit of the brain corresponds to heaven and the substance of the brain and its essence correspond to its matter. The faculty of imagination corresponds to the imprinted soul of the sphere; the imaginative forms correspond to the forms of things in the world of heaven prior to their existence in the external matters. The fourth one corresponds to the forms created in the external elemental matters.

The movement of the parts (of his body) corresponds to the movement of heaven; the existence of writing, etc., from human being in the external matter is the subject (or substrate) for his act. His art corresponds to the existence of the external generated beings in the elemental matters. The domination of the human intellect in the brain is like the domination of the Great Spirit in the Throne. The manifestation of his real heart, which is his rational soul, in the pine-shaped heart is like the manifestation of Universal Soul of the sphere in the sun, which is an image of God the Exalted in the world of spheres because it is the light of the heavens and earth in our world.

According to this (simile) the light of the sun corresponds to the 'lamp', 'its oil' is its specific form which would give light though the fire of the immaterial soul of the sun has not touched it. The sphere is like the 'glass' [405] and the matter like the 'niche'. The natural power pervading the corporeal world is 'the blessed tree'. It is neither from the Orient of the intellectual substances nor from the Occident of the material dimensions. 'The oil whereof would give light' and illuminates the corporeal lights, though the fire of the Universal Soul that constitutes them has not touched it, is the vicegerent of the Soul in the world of natures as the Souls and the Intellects are the vicegerents of God in the world of Spirit. 'Light upon light' means the sensible light from the sun is joined to the light of his non-material soul, or the light of his soul is the constituent for his sensible light and has superiority over it.

According to this interpretation, the sensible light for the body of the sun is a simile for the Necessary Light, which corresponds to the sun of the intellectual lights. In the rest of the real [or esoteric] interpretations that we have mentioned the sensible light is reckoned to be much more remote than the light of the heavens and the earth. Rather, it is reckoned to be the canvas, ashes and pen for the Words of God written by the Intellectual Pen on the Psychic Tablets, or on the external Allotments. As it is said in the following verse: The planet Mercury makes me a chimney, and from the smoke I feed the revolving lamp.

*Illuminations and Allusions (*Ishrāqāt wa Ishārāt*)*

The doors we opened for your heart by the permission of God and recited to you the Book of Wisdom, its essence of subtle mysteries concerning the issues of the knowledge of God, the great signs from the celestial scriptures, the origins of His creation and His generosity, the fruits of His mercy, and the rays of the sun of His generosity [the matters concerning the Perfect Man] must have become clear to you. If one is sagacious he will observe carefully man's kingdom (*mamlakat al-ādamīyi*, i.e. the totality of human body and his soul), the penetration of his command in his faculties and instruments (or perceptive organs), his encompassing the knowledge which is in his world, the levels of his existents, the pervasion of his light in his forms of knowledge and its perceptual imprints obtained in the mirror of his essence, which are then inscribed on the tablets of his representations, which [406] correspond to his world of heavens; then they get inhered in his material and corporeal substrata which correspond to his world of earth and its generated beings. He will then see by this very illumination that his spiritual ipseity is the locus of manifestation of the Divine Invisible Ipseity; that his psychic ipseity is the locus of manifestation of the (Divine) Name 'Allah', and the similitude of His light penetrates in his heaven and earth. Then he will truly understand the meaning of the Light Verse (*āyat al-nūr*) in the deepest sense with certainty. And he will know through the knowledge of luminous vision and the illuminative unveiling (knowledge) by presence that indeed God is the Light of the heavens and the earth.

Everything that is found in the human domain and in his world, its existence and manifestation is by the light of his ipseity which is invisible from the people owing to the intensity of the manifestation of its traces, the multiplicity of its acts and lights. So its acts and traces become a veil for the people [preventing them] from seeing its essence and witnessing its beauty and majesty, just as the manifestation of macrocosm and the loci of manifestation of the Divine Names are a veil for the people [preventing them] from seeing the Exalted Lord, His Beauty and His Majesty. But it is through Him that earth and heaven are illuminated, and He is the Light by which the loci of manifestation of (His) Names are manifested.

In the same way, one's luminous intellectual essence, the perceptive intellectual, psychic, imaginative and sensory forms are obtained and unveiled in the levels of one's perceptive organs of pen, tablet, decree and allotment. Likewise, by the divine self-subsisting Essence everything that is in the worlds and realms is illuminated; the Tablets, the Allotments, the lands and the heavens subsist as manifest, visible, illumined and existentially actualized.

So praise be to the Lord for bestowing upon you a key to the treasures of His mercy and generosity, for 'with Him are the keys of the Invisible, none but He knows them' [6:59]. Rather, He is 'a hidden treasure' by which all desires and wishes are fulfilled, and 'they are in your selves, do you not see?' [51:21]; and precious pearls by which attaining every existent becomes easy; they are a ladder for ascending to the ascents of the reality, the Object of worship [which He shows] 'in themselves, until it is manifest to them that He is the Reality' [41:53].

[407] There is nothing that is not found in man. There is no effort that it is impossible to realize by the one who deeply contemplates on it. He is the great talisman, the antidote capable of removing the poison, the great criterion [to discern right from wrong], the threshold to the wisdom of lights of God, the 'clear book' [12:1], the hidden mystery, 'the awesome tidings concerning which they are in disagreement' [78:2–3], the spiritual meaning of the letters *kāf* and *nūn* [or *kun* meaning 'be', the divine command mentioned in the

Qur'ān, 2:117], the clear Qur'ān [15:1], the firm grip [2:256; 31:22], the strong rope, the repellent of devil, the night of power, the greatest name, the day of gathering (*Jum'ah*), the furthest mosque (*masjid al-Aqsà*), the Ka'bah, the sanctuary 'and the house frequented, and the roof uplifted and the sea swarming' [52:4–6], 'a fine parchment unrolled' [52:3], and other than these from his names and attributes, which cannot be enumerated and counted.

*Muḥammadan Wisdom (*Ḥikmat Muḥammadīyya*)*

O wayfarer, know, contemplate, reflect and consider what is written in these lines, and enlighten your eyes by the collyrium of the imprint of this Psalter; have certainty that the straight path and the way towards God the Noble is not on earth nor in heaven, neither on the land nor in the sea, neither in this world nor in the next world, but it is in the self (*dhāt*) of the wayfarer, going from within him towards his Lord: 'Say: this is my path: I call to God upon insight, I and whosoever follows me' [12:108].

Your cure is within you but you are unaware
Your curer is from you but you see not.

[The Perfect man] is the pen of the Primary Reality, the teacher of man for what he does not know, [as the Exalted says:] 'He has taught thee what thou knewest not [before]' [4:113]; he is a tablet of God taken by the hand of the prophets and [their] inheritors (*al-awṣiyā'*), as the Exalted says [about him]: 'he took up the tablets, and in their inscription there was guidance' [7:154], 'so take what the Messenger gives you' [59:7], for it is the clear Qur'ān, the strong rope of God. Indeed the Qur'ān is the character trait of the Perfect Man, as it is narrated by one of his [Muḥammad's] wives. [408] When asked about his character trait, peace be upon him and upon his progeny, she answered: 'His character trait was the Qur'ān.'

Everything that is in the earth and in the heavens is in this one named by all the names, because he is the clear book; everything whether humid or dry is in him; in him is the bounty and its pleasure; in him is hellfire and its tribulation, in him is life and death; in him is the reward and punishment; in him is a meadow from the meadows of Gardens; in him is a pit from the pits of hellfires, as I said in the following rhyming couplets (*mathnawī*):

> Within is a meadow from Paradise, within is a pit from fire-temple
> In it is the heart which they build, so every moment the beloved ones visit it,
> The angels circumambulate it with admiration, as around the tomb of the great ones
> But there is another heart full of curse, wildness, filth and worms like the tomb of a Jew[1]
> Full of obscenity, evil whispering, greed, lies, it has not taken enkindling from the lights of wisdom.
> One is the tablet from writing of hidden knowledge, one is the letter full of evil whispering and suspicion
> On that copy the writing of reality was written, on this one the hand of Satan struck the pen.[2]

O God I take refuge in Thee from the grave, and the source of the torture of the grave whose cause is the human condition (*al-basharīyya*), which is full of torture. Whoever is not liberated from it is not liberated from the torture of the grave, so 'turn ye to your Lord' [39:54] 'and be quick for forgiveness from your Lord' [3:133]. A certain great [mystic] was asked about the torture in the grave and he replied: 'The grave, all of it, is torture.'

1. By 'Jew' Ṣadrā – according to a then widespread theological conception of Judaism – means one who is a sinner and who has deviated from the path leading to God. Cf. his '*Tafsīr sūrah al-Fātiḥah*', in *Tafsīr al-Qur'ān al-Karīm*, vol. 1, p. 144.
2. Ṣadrā has composed a number of rhyming couplets (*mathnawī*) and quatrains in Persian, some of which were published together with his *Se Aṣl*, edited by S. H. Nasr, and the entire available collection in *Majmū-i Ash'ār*, edited by M. Khājawī.

Know that the first level from the levels of wayfaring towards God is the exit from the strait of the world – the grave of human condition, the dust of psychic forms. It is given in a tradition from the Messenger of God, peace of God be upon him and upon his progeny: 'If any one desires to look at a walking dead then let him look at me.'[1] The first thing that is unveiled to him from the states of the next world and about which he is informed is the states of the dead ones, the unveiling of the graves, the actualization of what is in the breasts and what the imagination conceives for the dead in it from the snakes, [409] scorpions, dogs, torturous pernicious things, the interrogation by [the two angels] Munkar and Nakīr.[2]

This is also difficult to perceive by the masters of hairsplitting arguments and discursive reason, by the reasons of philosophers, naturalists and materialists, because it is beyond the levels of their reasons. They are not satisfied like the rest of the people [who follow] in such matters by sheer unreflective imitation (*al-taqlīd*). That is because they are wary of accepting anything without a rational proof. But there is no rational proof for the matters pertaining to spiritual witnessing and unveiling. So they are taken by surprise [when they hear these matters] and say: 'How can it be possible that a man is interrogated and addressed in his grave; the two angels descend upon him; the man witnesses them; they address him; he hears their words, whereas other than the dead do not see them, and do not hear anything from them?' Now in this station there is a great mystery,[3] and it is not permissible to reveal that except to the one whose attachment to the world [i.e. the lower passions] is severed and his spirit has exited from this tenebrous grave.

Anyway the aim that is being pursued (here) is, the Perfect Man is the sum total of what is in the macrocosm from the substances and

1. *Aḥādith-i Mathnawī*, no. 616.
2. See our article on 'Mullā Ṣadrā on Imaginative Perception and Imaginal World', in *Transcendent Philosophy*, vol. 1:2, pp. 81–96, in which we have discussed the imaginative realm and its creation.
3. On this issue see our article on 'Reincarnation or Resurrection …' *op. cit.*

accidents, heaven, earth and stars, angel, jinn and animal, Garden and Fire, the Book, the Path, the Balance, etc. He is the vicegerent of God on earth and in heaven. He has the substance, which is his essence, and the accidents, which are his qualities. The heaven is his head, the stars are his senses, the sun is his heart, the earth is his body, the mountains are his bones, the birds are his perceptive faculties and the wild beasts are his powers inciting [evil]. Nay, everything that God has brought into existence in the two worlds, the physical and the celestial, is commanded to obey the Perfect Man and prostrate before him because he is the vicegerent of the Exalted Lord, the locus of manifestation of all [divine] Names, as He says: 'And He has subjected you to what is in the heavens and what is in the earth' [45:13] and 'He has lavished on you His blessings, externally and internally' [31:20]. So, all the atoms of the two realms of generated beings glorify him as they glorify God the Exalted. It is recorded in a tradition: 'Whatever is in the heavens and the earth, even the fish in the sea, asks for atonement of the learned.'

So all the inhabitants of the celestial and physical worlds, all the angels of God were commanded together by [410] God: 'prostrate yourselves to Man (*ādam*)' [2:34] to obey this vicegerent of the Lord and the glorified mystery. He has two vicegerencies: minor and major. When God the Exalted desires by His complete power and perfect wisdom to make someone His vicegerent on earth of the creatures, and a deputy to be sent from His presence to unveil the truths, reveal the spiritual meanings, spread the good far and wide, He makes the earth and everything in it subjected to him so that the causes for the minor, external sovereignty are gathered for him. It is said: 'The sovereign is the shadow of God on the lands.'

He subjected him to what is in heaven so that the instruments of his major sovereignty are collected together. He built for him a physical bed in the 'frequented house' [52:4] of the heart in the kingdom of body and the world of the physical mould. Then He commanded the angels of the lower [world] to obey and follow him by saying: 'prostrate before Man'. So under his feet everything that was in the earth of the body prostrated, [such as] the mountains of bones, the waters of mouth, eyes and ears, the climes of seven external limbs, i.e. the two arms, two feet, back, stomach and head, the stars of the senses, the hell of the intestine, the guards of hell of the natural powers, the throne of the heart, the footstool of the breast, the heavens of the mind full of intellectual inspirations and cognitive meanings coming from the direction of the luminous subtle light corresponding to the highest plenum for this vicegerent, and the lowest plenum corresponding to the devils and the enemies of God, the breath coming out from his interior corresponding to matter receptive to the simple forms and their composites; the letters of the alphabet corresponding to the simple forms of species of spheres and elements; the three words [in grammar], noun, verb and preposition, corresponding to three kingdoms, mineral, plant and animal.

When this minor vicegerency was completed for him, God assisted him with the soldiers who cannot be [physically] seen for the major vicegerency. By these spiritual soldiers he subjected for him everything that is in the physical and celestial worlds according to His saying: 'And He subjected you to what is in the heavens and what is in the earth' [45:13]. Then He commanded the angels of both realms of beings to obedience to this deputy of the Lord and prostration to this vicegerent of God. So all of the angels prostrated before him. By this the deputyship of the world of creation and command completed for him, He says: 'Verily His are the creation and the command' [7:54], 'so blessed be God, the best of creators'` [23:14].

*Elaboration of Discourse for the Clarification of Station (*Basṭ Kalām li-Tawḍīḥ Maqām*)*

[411] This lordly threshold, the most proximate servant to the Sublime, the vicegerent of God the Exalted, the mirror for the forms of things is above the two realms of beings for two reasons:

complete knowledge of the realities of things [as they are] and the perfect power over what he wills.

As for knowledge, it is divided into his knowledge of the external [world] and knowledge of the internal [world].

By his external knowledge he encompasses what is needed for him for his external vicegerency, such as: how to deduce the arts, how to use the natures, the knowledge of subjugating the animals and hunting the beasts and birds on the earth and in the air; bringing out the fish from the depths of the oceans through the [use] of the power of deliberation; bringing down the birds from the high atmosphere by the [use of] subtle reflection and sound discernment; hunting down the beasts from the summit of the mountain and hills by multiple tricks; deducing the measures of spheres and their depths by extreme wit and subtle understanding; to know through the knowledge of travelling and the power of swimming the constellations, the formation of the stars, their measures, motions and directions; the climes of the earth and the measures of the mountains; the judgment on the eclipse of the moon and the sun in determined times and known moments; the enactment of some sciences, such as the sciences of literatures, *sharī'ah* (the divine Law), ethics and morality; political science and the science of government, the science of astronomy and medicine, of language and poetry, of arithmetic and music, of omen, divination, conjuring, physiognomy, stratagem, drawing weights, digging canals, the science of the substances and minerals, pharmacology, mineralogy – both in units and compositions - curing the sick of malady and poison, the science of farming and agriculture, and the rest of the artisan sciences.

His inner knowledge consists of the knowledge of spiritual entities and of the unveiling of the angels of the higher world, knowledge of the intellectual substances and Platonic Ideas, the primary [412] principles and the most Primary Principle, the ultimate goals and the most Ultimate Goal. In brief, it is the knowledge of God, His angels, His Books, His messengers, the Last Day, and the intellectual intuition (*iḥāṭah*) of the Form of existence of all. By this man becomes as if one of the inhabitants of the region of the Lord and a subject of the world of Intellect.

As for the power, its completion manifests in the second mode of existence. There will result what he acquires here [in this mode of existence], [as the Exalted said:] 'Therein shall you have what your souls desire' [41:31], and in that [state] he will witness the confining of the angels and their obedience to the Perfect Man as obedience to God, as He said: 'Prostrate yourselves to Man (*ādam*)' [2:34]. In this [command] his vicegerency to God was realized in reality, and this is the mystery of His saying: 'When I have fashioned him [in due proportion] and blown into him My spirit, fall ye down, prostrating yourselves unto him' [15:29].

*Philosophical Foundation on which the Principles of Gnosis are Based (*Asās Ḥikmī Yubtanā 'alayhi Uṣūl 'Irfānīyya*)*

The fundamental realities have realms and modes of existence, the loci of manifestations and similitudes, all of which are found in the human 'comprehensive mosque' (*al-masjid al-jāmi'*, i.e. the Perfect Man). He is the temple of the people who remember and glorify [God], and the locus of worship of all creatures. One of the (fundamental realities) is the Garden (or Paradise). His beautiful character-trait is the extension of the Garden whose breadth is like the breadth of the firmament and the earth; his evil character-trait is the narrowness of its hellfire; his beautiful acts are the forms of the Garden, such as the rivers, the *houris* and palaces; his ugly acts are the form of Fires, snakes and harmful things, boiling water and the infernal tree. These are the attributes and habits both beautiful and ugly, and acts and traces both good and evil. They are the root of what the man will witness in the next world, and the seed of what will come to exist and actualize in the next world which will be an existence and an actualization more complete and more stable than the existence of these material worldly forms, and by which the fortunate ones will be blessed and the wretched ones will be tortured by those that are the contraries (of the forms of the fortunate ones).

The people of the Garden have power over bringing to presence what they like [to eat] and to obtain their taste. They have in it what they invite, which descends from the Most Forgiving [413] Most Merciful [as in His words]: 'Therein shall be all the objects of the souls' appetite and the eyes' delight' [43:71]. So much so that the lowliest among the people of the Garden and the most feeble among them eat in a moment without exhaustion and fatigue a measure of what all the people of the world eat, and they find in one morsel the pleasure of seventy flavours from the flavours of the [food in this] world and their sweetness. This is the Garden of the common people, including the feeble-minded ones and others.[1]

As for the Garden of the lovers of God, it is what is expressed in the saying of the Exalted: 'Thou enter among My servants and enter in my Garden' [89:30]; and [in a sacred tradition]: 'It is prepared for my virtuous servants what no eye has seen, what no ear has heard and what has never passed into the heart of any mortal.'[2]

In sum, these higher levels of the Garden and their contraries which are the descending lower levels of hellfire are present within man in this world but the people are heedless of these two [i.e. the Garden and the hellfire and their levels] except the one whom God helps with complete unveiling. Then he sees what others see (and also 'sees') what lies within their hide (or within themselves), which they themselves do not see for 'they call from a far place' [41:44]. Whereas 'for the righteous, the Garden is brought near to them and for those

1. Here Ṣadrā intends the intermediate realm of the soul (*al- 'ālam al-barzakh*) or the imaginal world and the creative imagination of the soul (to use H. Corbin's terminology). Cf. H. Corbin, *En Islam iranien*, vol. iv, pp. 106–122. Corbin has translated and analysed Ṣadrā's glosses on the sections in *The Philosophy of Illumination, op. cit.*, which deal with the World of Imagination and the body of resurrection or the imaginal body of the soul.
2. *Aḥādith-i Mathnawī*, no. 264.

straying in evil, the hellfire is placed in full view of them' [26:90–91]; 'and they will not be absent from them' [82:16].

Know that the Exalted Reality is one God, the one All-provider, the All-unfolding one. From Him one emanation descends, which pervades in all in the same measure coming from Him, but it differs according to the difference in tastes and drinking vessels. As the Exalted said: 'We cause the rain to descend from the sky' [15:22] and 'watered with the same water yet some of them We make more excellent than others to eat' [13:4]. So from it is the sweet water of Euphrates owing to the purity of the substratum and the healthy heart; and from it is the bitter saline water owing to the impurities of the substratum because of the sins and misdeeds.

The comprehensive name for the common Garden and Fire in all the degrees is existent in the macrocosm and microcosm, and beyond the two is 'the union with the Beloved' or 'the separation from Him'. So, the Garden in reality for the fortunate ones is their attaining what they desire most and what they love, for 'therein shall be all the objects of the souls' appetite' [43:71]. [414] The hellfire of the wretched ones is their separation from the desirable things of the world and futile pleasures, for 'between them and what they desire is placed a barrier' [34:54]. As for the Garden of the proximate ones it is witnessing their Object of worship, whose contrary is to be veiled [from Him], which is the hellfire for the distant ones [according to His saying]: 'Verily that Day they shall be veiled from their Lord' [83:15].

Some lover has said: 'Love is the way, and the vision of the beloved is the Garden, the separation [from the beloved] is the Fire which is "the Fire of God [kindled] to a blaze that rises up to the hearts"' [104:7].

Know that the path of the lovers and their way is other than the paths of [common] people and their ways. The movement of the lovers and their striving is other than the movements of the [common] people and their strivings in action and in seeking a goal. For the movement of the lovers is the divine attraction which corresponds to the act of two scales; the goal of their striving, their journey and the end of their movements is meeting God the Exalted; their hellfire is being veiled from Him. They desire the Garden and that which makes proximate to it in speech and in act, for in them are the shadows of His Face and the ray of the light of His Beauty [as the proverb goes:] '[when selecting a house for living] look for a [good] neighbour [first], then the house.'

What is discerned in this claim is [for instance] that the vision of the sun is something, and the vision of its rays is something else, but the sun is not known and one cannot be guided towards it except through the rays. This is the similitude of the desire of a gnostic for things, and his obedience to the one Who is other than him. There is another similitude, clearer than the former, given by the people of reflection and imagination: the vision of the moon in the water is something, and seeing the face of the moon on the night of the full moon is another thing; but whoever sees the face of the moon in the water has seen it except that he sees it with the veil of his estimation. Likewise the heart of the gnostic is like the mirror in which the mystery of God is seen, as a certain [gnostic] said: 'The similitude of the heart is like the mirror, when a man looks into it his Lord self-manifests Himself.'

In the book of Ibn Mas'ūd, may God be pleased with him, it is given: 'The similitude of His light in the heart of the one who has faith is like a niche in which is a lamp.' So look at the difference between the enlightened heart in which the light of the Face of God is witnessed and the tenebrous inverted heart which is the nest of Devil [as the Exalted said]: 'And when the Word is fulfilled against them, We shall bring forth for them out of earth a Beast that shall speak unto them' [27:82].

[415] Let us return to what we were discussing earlier. [I hope] the people of sound intellect will forgive me [for digressing] for indeed

one discourse has led me to another and has made us arrive at this place. Our discourse was: The realities have similitude in (all) the worlds. Rather, the constitution of every realm is [based] on the existence of the loci of manifestation and similitudes. All the forms of this world are the similitude of what is in the highest world; they manifest to the human soul through the mirrors of the senses and the loci of manifestation of the perceptions. Rather, for anyone who is in one of the worlds, that world will be the world of manifestation before him, present to him and the other than (that world) is invisible to him and veiled from his observation. [In the majority of cases] the people's confidence and reliance is on the affirmation of the forms existent in this world and not the forms existent in the other world, which is higher than this world because of their getting mixed up with the senses and their mingling with the objects of senses. But the gnostics are different from them.

It is narrated from the Commander of the Faithful ['Alī ibn Abī Ṭālib], peace be upon him, that he said: 'I am more aware of the states of the heavens than the states of the earth;'[1] and the saying of the Prophet, peace be upon him and upon his progeny: 'Heaven made a lot of noise and it had every reason to do so because there is no place, even of one foot, but there is [an angel] in prostration and in genuflection in it.'[2] From this it is quite clear that he, peace be upon him and upon his progeny, had known the states of every heaven inch by inch, as well as what was connected to it from soul and intellect, and expressed the two as prostrating and in genuflection.

The reliance of the laity and the externalists (*ẓāhiriyyūn*) from among the scholars of religion is upon the forms of this world because of their inability to separate every form from all the material properties. If a form to which they adhere is separated from some material properties, it becomes doubtful for them so they deny

1. Cf. *Nahj al-Balāghah*, part 2, p. 130. The text in this work varies. Instead of 'states' it mentions 'pathways'.
2. *Aḥādith-i Mathnawī*, no. 377.

it because of their intimacy with the particular matter and their reliance upon sensible forms. But, for someone who is learned and well-grounded [in matters of intellect or spirit], when [he sees] [416] a form he purifies the substance from the matter and makes it an existence purified from the wrappings [of forms], so it becomes most real to him, most stable and most lasting.

*[Divine] Assistance (*Ta'yīd*)*

You must have heard what is reported from the Prophet, peace be upon him and upon his progeny, that he said: 'There is a market in the Garden [or Paradise] in which the forms are bought.'[1] It is narrated from one of the pious persons who said: 'I saw my Lord in a dream in the form of my mother.'[2] An interpreter interpreted the 'Lord' as the verses of the Qur'ān and the 'mother' as the Prophet, peace be upon him and upon his progeny, for with him is the 'essence of the Book'. This is one kind of similitude. The Prophet, peace be upon him and upon his progeny, at times saw Gabriel in the form of an Arab nomad, at times in the form of Diḥyā al-Kalbī, and at times in a gigantic form as if it covered from East to West.[3] All these are different [kinds] of conceptualizations (*al-tamthīlāt*) according to various [spiritual] stations and different modes of existence [of the Prophet], for Gabriel is one reality but [seen] differently according to the different worlds and modes of existence [of a person].[4]

---

1. It is taken over from Ibn 'Arabī, *Futūḥāt al-Makkīyya*, vol. 2, p. 628. Here Ṣadrā states the crucial role of the faculty of imagination, which is non-material according to him. See our article on 'Mullā Ṣadrā on Imaginative Perception and Imaginal World', *op. cit.*
2. *Tamhīdāt, op. cit.*, p. 296.
3. Cf. Bukhārī, *op. cit.*, vol. 1: the 'Book of Revelation' in which he reports some traditions of the Prophet concerning various ways in which he received the divine revelations.
4. Cf. our article on 'Mullā Ṣadrā on Imaginative Perception and Imaginal World', *op. cit.*

According to this analogy there are the narratives recorded in connection with the Prophet, peace be upon him and upon his progeny, about his seeing His Lord, and the seeing of the rest of the prophets and the friends [of God,] peace be upon them, the Lord in different modes, variegated in visibility and invisibility in accordance with the thickness and subtlety of the veil [of their perception].

One of the veils is the ego (*al-huwīyya*, lit. ipseity) of the wayfarer, [as it said:] 'The existence [of your ego] is a sin; no sin can be compared with it;'[1] and his determined [state] called 'the mount of Moses', peace be upon him. So long as the wayfarer's ego is not annihilated and the mountain of his determined [or fixed] state (*ta'ayyun*) [of mind] is not removed and dissolved, as solid ice is dissolved by melting at the rise and the power of the real sun on it, he cannot not witness the Exalted Divine Essence. Hence the first thing incumbent upon the wayfarer, the traveller towards God with veracious feet and knowledge, is to remove from his way the torture of his ego, which is among those that set [like the stars, the moon and the sun]. Then when he develops gradually in his levels from the form of nature, to the soul and then to the intellect, [417] it would be like [seeing] the stars [first], then the moon and then the sun. Only then he will affirm veraciously as did Khalīl [i.e. the prophet Abraham] that 'I have turned my face to Him who originated the heavens and the earth as a true believer (*ḥanīf*) and the one surrendered (*muslim*), and never shall I be a polytheist' [6:79].

One of the marks of friendship (*walāyah*) with God the Exalted is the desire for death, as He the Glorified said: 'O ye who are Jews, if you claim that you are friends of God apart from (all) mankind, then long for death if you are truthful' [62:6].

Among the wayfarers travelling towards God the Exalted the one who complained (most) from his heart, spirit and the innermost

1. J. Nurbakhsh has recorded this saying in his *Traditions of the Prophet*, no. 45. This collection also contains some oft-quoted sayings of the Shī'ite Imams and Ṣūfīs.

consciousness about the torture of his ego, necessary for every one surrendered [to the will of God, (*muslim*)] to get rid of its torture according to the requisite of his surrender from the way of the surrendered ones, was Abū Yazīd Bastāmī.[1] He said: 'The human condition is an obstacle to lordship, so from whomsoever is veiled by the human condition, lordship has slipped away.'[2] Likewise, Ḥusayn ibn Manṣūr [al-Ḥallāj] said:

> Kill 'me' O my trustworthy friends, for in the killing of 'me' is my life.[3]

Do you not see that those who have faith praise God and thank Him for their liberation from the human condition as God narrates about them by His saying: 'Praise be to God Who has put grief away from us, surely our Lord is Oft-Forgiving, Ever-Responsive [to gratitude]' [35:34].

*Reminder (*Tadhkirah*)*

Know that the knowledge of the states of dead ones and remembrance of death are among the greatest of worships. The veil of the human condition is the greatest of all the veils [over such knowledge], and its lifting is one of the most important affairs. That is why God tests the hearts of people to see if they long for it [or not] as He says: 'Long for death if you are truthful' [62:6]; and according to a tradition from (the Prophet), peace be upon him and upon his progeny: 'The hearts become rusty as iron becomes rusty.

1. Abū Yazīd al-Bastāmī (d. c. 261/874) was one of the early Ṣūfīs, famous for his paradoxical utterances (*shaṭḥīyyāt*), like the ones that Ṣadrā quotes here, which were contemplated and commentated by many subsequent generations of Ṣūfīs and Muslim sages. Some of his sayings are compiled in Rūzbihān Baqlī's *Sharḥ-e Shaṭḥīyyāt*, edited by H. Corbin.
2. *Tamhīdāt*, *op. cit.*, p. 298.
3. Schimmel, in her *Mystical Dimensions of Islam*, p. 69, quotes this famous verse of Ḥallāj and also gives a summary of his biography.

Their polish is the remembrance of death and the recitation of the Qur'ān."[1]

[418] If you ask for the truth, [then know that] the rust of human condition and the limitation of the fixed state [of mind], which are like the action of two heavy scales, do not vanish from the hearts except through some attraction from God. Reflect on this matter that the mirror of the heart of the 'master of mankind' [i.e. the Prophet Muḥammad, peace be upon him], the most noble among the contingent [beings], could not become clean from the rusts of inclinations and the coverings of attentions to this world [by itself] so he needed to ask for the forgiveness [of God] seventy times a day and night, as given in a famous tradition, in order to protect the station of proximity and servitude [to God].[2] So who could clean the mirror [of his heart] and purify his essence completely from the [base] human qualities by mere acquisition [of knowledge] and action without divine attraction!

The saying of a certain Shaykh is not far from [the above view] as he said: 'The purifier (*al-ṣūfī*) is indeed God',[3] which alludes to this matter. That is to say, the purification (*al-taṣawwuf*) and separation from bondage to the carnal soul (*nafs*) [leading to evil] and servitude to the appetite, and complete turning to the reality is obtained only by the generosity of God and His help to the wayfarer who is steadfast on His strong rope. It is as if God were casting the inspirations one after the other in his heart, and shedding gnosis (*ma'ārif*) in regular succession on the innermost recess of his soul (*sirr*) in order to drag him out from becoming accustomed to the world of human condition and into the world of the Lord. That is the meaning (*ma'nī*) of His saying: 'And We taught him knowledge from Us' [18:65].

1. *Tamhīdāt, op. cit.*, p. 299.
2. *Aḥādith-i Mathnawī*, no. 425.
3. *Tamhīdāt, op. cit.*, p. 313.

From this it becomes clear that worship without knowledge has neither measure nor worth. The effort of anyone without knowledge is like (giving) movements to the dead and minerals in which there is neither purpose nor meaning, nor gain in it, like accidental motion. Every motion's goal is the genus of its origin as it is evident through analogy and induction. It has been proved that the goal is precisely the same as the agent in the perfect way. If the principle of the motion is natural then its goal will be something natural, like arriving at the natural field. If it is something pertaining to animal condition then its goal will be something pertaining to animal condition, like eating, drinking, concupiscence and vengeance. If its principle is spiritual then its goal will be to arrive at the celestial world, like gnosis of the next world; if it is something divine, then its goal will be the closeness to and a way-station with God by the annihilation of the ego-consciousness (*al-nafs*) [419] and the subsistence (of the soul without ego-consciousness) by its Principle and Goal.

If God had not ordered His servant [to wake up], and the inviter to the reality had not permitted him to enter His threshold and arrive at His side [which He indicates] in His symbolic 'O thou enwrapped in thy robes' [73:1], who would have risen from his sleep in order to pray most of the night and fast the whole day! The Messenger of God, peace be upon him and upon his progeny, used to stay awake at night [in the remembrance of God] and remain thirsty during the day before being sent [as the Messenger]. He used to stand in worship in the [cave of] mount Hira until his feet swelled; and he used to say: 'The dearest thing to me is prayer.'[1] That is because his utmost intimacy was with the remembrance of God, and His worship was for the sake of His gnosis and knowledge by the fruit of servitude. This was [to lead him to] the Divine Goal. So 'worship thy Lord until the certainty comes to thee' [15:99].

Thus God, may He be Glorified, was the One Who stirred him, was his Inviter, the One Who reared him, and was his Shepherd and

1. *Aḥādīth-i Mathnawī*, no. 182.

nothing else neither of this world nor of the next. That is why God called him 'orphan' in His saying: 'Did He not find thee an orphan and gave thee shelter?' [93:6], that is, (he was given shelter) in the Garden of Sanctity (*quds*), in the neighbourhood of God and in His proximity. He alludes to it in his, peace be upon him and upon his progeny, saying: 'I and the guardian of the orphan are like these two [fingers] in the Garden',[1] and he brought his index and middle fingers together. In other words, this world is the station of cattle and beasts [as it is said:]: 'This world is a corpse, its seekers are dogs.'[2] For how can the shelter become the refuge of the noblest creation of God! The world is like a station of a rider and like a vanishing shadow, 'it is a house for the one who has no house'. There is a tradition from him, peace be upon him and upon his progeny [which states]: 'The similitude of me and the similitude of [my being in] the world are like a rider who takes shelter in the shade of a tree. After having rested, he leaves it.'[3] The Messenger of God, peace be upon him and upon his progeny, came to this world for the guidance of mankind and their liberation [from the soul which incites to evil] [as He said:] 'There has come to you from God a light and a manifest Book' [5:15], and His saying: 'We have not sent thee save as a mercy unto all the worlds' [21:107].

*Admonishing Reminder (*Dhikr Tanbīhī*)*

Nay, we say that the Mover of all existents is the Creator, may His remembrance be majestic, by His love pervading [420] in all particles, but some through the intermediary of the other. The Exalted said: 'Surely your Lord is God Who created the heavens and the earth in six days, then He sat upon the Throne, covering the night with the day, which is in haste to follow it, and He made the sun and the moon and the stars subservient to His command' until His saying: 'Blessed be God, the Lord of all worlds' [7:54].

1. *Tamhīdāt, op. cit.*, p. 302.
2. *Aḥādith-i Mathnawī*, no. 705.
3. *Tamhīdāt, op. cit.*, p. 307.

Know that the cosmos, all of it, is like one person who dances according to his different positions, different modes of the motions of his parts, some of which are fast, some are slow, some have little motion, some are in repose. Its external dimension dances, and its internal dimension quivers in different modes of dancing and quivering according to natural, psychic and intellectual motions for different wishes and variegated purposes ranking in degrees from low to high. It seeks proximity to the different principles in loftiness, nobility and beauty until it ends at the next divine Goal for the first Active Principle, transcending all deficiency and effervescence, which is the receptive subject of Muḥammad, may the noblest peace and perfect mercies be upon him and upon his progeny. The salutations and mercies correspond to different hierarchical forms of the subject of motion. It is said for its description: 'It is the first perfection for that which is potentiality *qua* potentiality.'

So infer from it the state of the goal, the agent and the receptacle, and realize the truth of the saying of the one who said: 'Indeed, he who claims that Muḥammad saw his Lord, he has fabricated a great lie for God.'

*Banishing Doubt (*Izāḥat Shakk*)*

If whatever has been mentioned is comprehended then the doubts of contradiction [should have] banished from you.

There is another explanation which the saying of the Prophet, peace be upon him and upon his progeny, clarifies. [He said]: 'It was a Light that I saw', and also the saying of the Commander of the Faithful ['Alī ibn Abī Ṭālib], peace be upon him [who said]: 'I saw Him, then I worshipped Him, [421] I would not worship a Lord whom I did not see.'[1] In the context of the divine vision there are two sayings narrated from him [i.e. the Prophet], peace be upon him

1. *Uṣūl al-Kāfī*, vol. 1, p. 131, no. 259.

and his progeny, though apparently there is mutual contradiction in them. One, his saying to some of his wives: 'I saw my Lord in His I-ness and Reality', and the other his saying, peace be upon him, to Ibn 'Abbās: 'I saw Him in the imaginal Form'. There are other sayings [of the Prophet] in the context of the imaginal Form such as: 'The first thing that God created was my light',[1] and 'he who has seen me has indeed seen the reality'.[2]

Through its explanation, which we have established, and its foundation, which we have strongly confirmed, the truth of the saying of the pillars of the philosophy is evident: 'The speaker and the judge of this [proposition] that "God is existent" gives a kind of demonstration resembling "causal demonstration" not rational demonstration.' His saying, peace be upon him and upon his progeny, confirms that: 'Reflect upon the instruments of God but reflect not upon God's Essence.'[3] That is because the reflection, (even if) total, does not have the power [to encompass] the Creator. [As He said:] 'They cannot encompass Him by knowledge, all faces are humbled unto Him the Living the Eternal' [20:111], for it is impossible for anyone to reach the Ground of the Essence of the Exalted and encompass it because none can penetrate it, that is to say, none can penetrate to that station, [for] 'the sights perceive Him not, but He perceives the sights' [6:103]. Therefore, [none] can see His Essence but His Essence.

It is given in one of the prophetic prayers: 'By Thee I am alive, by Thee I die'. From this the saying of Dhū'l-Nūn al-Misrī becomes clear: 'I saw my Lord by my Lord, for without my Lord I would not have had the power to see my Lord;'[4] and the saying of Ḥusayn al-Manṣūr [al-Ḥallāj]: 'None can see my Lord save my Lord.'

---

1. *Aḥādith-i Mathnawī*, no. 342.
2. *Ibid.*, no. 163.
3. *Ibid.*, no. 439.
4. *Tamhīdāt, op. cit.,* pp. 306, 330.

Conclusion and Testament (*Khatm wa Waṣīyya*)

[422] O my beloved, I have already mentioned to you the treasures of realities and symbols of subtle points in these sections. So know their worth and penetrate their depth; safeguard them from the wretched souls ignorant of the realities of faith, those who have no faith in the blessings of God because they are the enemies of wisdom, the rejecters of gnosis and lovers of caprice and devilry.

Know that the representation of realities in the form of words and in the garb of expressions and metaphors is but a sip from the wine jug; nay it is like a drop from a fathomless sea, or like rays from the sun. I have affirmed to you these meanings for two reasons: first [to caution you that], 'the vilest of mankind are those whose [life is geared to] eating only',[1] second, I have hope in the manifestation and emergence of one of my spiritual offspring from the people of spiritual proximity who will know the worth of these gnostic sciences, who is disengaged from the cover of these evil contemporaries and their malicious views. So make stable their seeds in the earth of your heart even though they may be above your level [of perception]. It is up to you and to them to taste the meanings of these words through purified souls, clear minds, cleansed hearts and attentive ears, for the best of the hearts are the most cleansed and the best of the ears are those that listen most and are most attentive.

1. *Tamhīdāt, op. cit.*, p. 90, 310.

God the Exalted said [those who did not listen to His guidance said]: 'Had we but listened and intellected [or reflected] we would not have been dwellers in the flames' [67:10]. Distance from the flames [and listening and reflecting on the meaning of these words] indeed comes through ascetic practice (*al-zuhd*) in the world and leaving [the worldly attachment] to those attached to it and engaged in it.

Know that him who leans and inclines towards the world God burns by His Fire, and he becomes the dust blown away by [423] the wind, for He is Most Powerful over everything. That is the quality of the lords of worldly kingdom and worldly people. Him who leans and inclines towards the next world God burns by His Fire, and he becomes pure gold from which one gets benefit. This is the quality of the people of the next world and the lords of the celestial kingdom, the people of the Garden. Him who leans and inclines towards God, God burns by His Light, and he becomes a priceless unique jewel, and a perfect pearl which has no similitude in this world and the next. This is the quality of the people of God, His loved ones and His friends.

I have mentioned to you that there are three worlds and three modes of existence: the world of sense or this world; the invisible world or the next world; the sacred world or the Refuge. The wayfarers are of three types: one type wayfares in this world, his capital is worldly goods and wealth, his gain is sins and regret; one type wayfares in the next world, his capital is worship, his gain is the Garden; one type wayfares towards God the Exalted, his capital is gnosis, his gain is meeting God.

Know that knowledge is the root of every felicity and ignorance is the foundation of every misery. The felicity of every mode of existence and world lies in the awareness of what is in it. In this world and whatever is in it, despite its being paltry, lowly and futile, still man gains pleasure if he has reached in maturity in (his) senses and become powerful in his animal organs of awareness. For every pleasure is due to obtaining the agreeable thing from the point of what is agreeable to him and the pain is its loss or obtaining what is contrary to him.

If the joy and pleasure in this lower world depend on its knowledge and awareness [by a person], then what do you surmise about the next world, which subsists on the intentions and gnosis! Further, what do you surmise about the Sacred world, which is the mine of the intellects and the source of gnosis! So you must have wisdom and gnosis.

As for asceticism, piety (*taqwā*) and the rest of the services [or worships of the Divine] and spiritual disciplines, all these are for the preparation of [obtaining divine] wisdom and are an introduction to [divine] gnosis. They are for the purification of the inner [self], the refinement of the innermost recess of the soul, for the polishing of the mirror of the heart from the covering and rust so that it becomes clean, and by which one can stand parallel to the reality and see in it [424] the Face of the Object of desire. As for the purification and polishing in themselves, this matter is something private (and) not the object of intention in principle. Rather, it is for the sake of what manifests through it or what is represented in it from the signs of the reality and the self-manifestation of His Face. But asceticism in the world, in whatever way it may be practised, is sheer nothing. An intelligent person will not practise asceticism for something that has no [eternal] value. There is a tradition of the Messenger, peace be upon him and upon his progeny, concerning this: 'If the world before God weighed the measure of the wings of a mosquito, He still would not quench the thirst of a person with no faith by drinking water from it',[1] the Qur'ān states: 'The life of this world is but an enjoyment of self-delusion' [3:185].

The period of the life of this world in comparison to the continuation of the next world is like a moment. The width of its

1. *Aḥādith-i Mathnawī*, no. 645.

place in comparison to the place of the next world is like an atom [as He said]: 'On the day when they behold it, it will be as if they have tarried for an evening, or its morn' [79:46]. There is a tradition from him, may peace be upon him and upon his progeny: 'What is the measure of (this) world compared with the next world but like the one who dips his finger in the ocean. Let him see what it brings out.'[1] So detachment from this insignificant thing [i.e. the worldly life] is necessary, which is possible only through asceticism in reality, because beyond it there is another world, nay other worlds, to which the purified souls return [as He said]: 'Surely the next world is greater in levels, and greater in preferment' [17:21].

He who desires to know the greatness of God and the greatness of His beautiful Names – whose shadows are the next world, and this world is the shadow of its shadows – and to find a greater share and abundant portion from His mercy, then let him abandon the next world and abandon the abandonment as well, so that he penetrates the depth [of his self and] arrives [before God] and is totally liberated from his ego (*nafs*) and his heart. It is said: 'Abandonment of the world makes the soul happy, abandonment of the next world makes the heart happy and turning totally towards God makes the spirit happy.'

Know that the existential worlds and the modes of existence correspond to a hierarchy of levels of which some encompass others. When the wayfarer rises from a world and enters into another world, it is as if he died in the previous one and is born in the next. Jesus, peace be upon him, said: 'He will not enter the celestial heavens unless he is born twice.'[2]

[425] One learns from this that the star [mentioned earlier in the verse of the Qur'ān], which is the form of nature and senses and is the first animal mode of existence, the moon, which is the form the soul and the first level of the human wayfarer, the sun, which is the

1. *Tamhīdāt, op. cit.*, p. 312.
2. *Aḥādith-i Mathnawī*, no. 273.

form of the intellect and is the final way-station of the world of contingents, all these are the indications of the forms of the three worlds. The wayfarer at the beginning of his wayfaring is in the first one of them according to the craving of his soul and its caprices. Then he dies to it voluntarily and enters the second one. Then his craving for it dies and he enters the celestial heavens according to His saying: 'Thus did We show Abraham the kingdom of the heavens and earth that he might be of those possessing certainty' [6:75]. Then his craving for all died, according to his saying: 'I love not the setters' [6:76]. He annihilated his [carnal] soul by his Lord, and turned the face of his self to the Originator of the heavens of intellects and the earth of souls, as a believer purified from the sins of being and ego (lit. ipseity) as a really surrendered one [to God], confessing His unity without associating anyone with Him. For as long as the ego of the wayfarer and its caprice have not vanished then they are the object of worship, the root of every worship and love for other than God, as His saying indicates: 'Have you seen him who takes his caprice as his god?' [25:43]. [Once he really surrenders to God] then the reality becomes the Efficient and Final [Causes] for him in every act, effort and movement; his own principles of motions from the perceptive faculties such as hearing and sight, and the movers such as hands and feet, whether they induce [to action] or are agents, are withdrawn.

Then [in this state] he says: 'My prayer and my sacrifice and my living and my dying are for God, the Lord of worlds' [6:162]; and he says: 'He who has seen me has indeed seen the reality'.[1] That is because the reality becomes his ear, his sight, his hand and his feet, as is given in the famous [sacred] tradition [of the Messenger].[2] That is because of the self-manifestation of the reality in the mirror of his heart. There is an indication to it in His saying: 'Our Lord, perfect

1. *Ibid.*, no. 163.
2. The reference is to the *ḥadīth qudsī* (sacred tradition) known as *ḥadīth al-nawāfil*, which states: 'My servant ceases not to draw nigh unto Me by supererogatory pious works, until I love him and when I love him I am the eye by which he sees, and the ear by which he hears, and the tongue by which he speaks, and the hand by which he grasps, and the foot by which he walks'. Cf. *Aḥādith-i Mathnawī*, no. 42.

our light for us' [66:8]; and His saying: 'Their light running before them, and on their right hands' [66:8]. One of the prophetic prayers is: 'O God, [426] grant me light in my heart, light in my hearing, light in my sight, light in my brain, light in my blood' until his saying: 'light in my hair, light in my bones, light in my grave'.[1] There is another [prophetic invocation] as well: 'O Light of lights! O Manager of affairs, O Knower of what is in the breasts!' That is the Light of His Face and His Essence, the Agent of all the existents. It is the Light of what is in the earth and in the heavens; the End of all goodness; the Goal of ascension of the existents. For 'the final end is unto thy Lord, and that He it is Who makes one laugh and makes one weep, and that He it is Who gives death and gives life, and He creates the two spouses, the male and the female from a sperm-drop when it is poured forth, and upon Him rests the second bringing forth' [53:42–43]; and by Him every believer believes, as 'God bears witness, and so do the angels and all who are endowed with knowledge that there is no god but Him, the Upholder of Equity' [3:18].

One of His Names is 'Supervising the believer'. If a believer severs his attention from his ego, from his belief, from his knowledge, from the well-known traces and remains without his ego, and comes to know that 'there is no he but He', then his belief is transformed to his experience (*'ayān*) [of the reality]; he emerges from the separation, and becomes annihilated in the (divine) witnessing. So what remains is the Sovereign of the existence, the Day which belongs to God the One, the Victorious; then his essence bears witness to His Essence in Absolute Unity, in pure Uniqueness saying that 'There is no god but Him' [3:18]. His essence also bears witness [to the Divine Unity] by the tongue of the angels, and those possessed of knowledge that rightness and justice subsist through Him, that He is the Reality of realities by His abiding Face, and all the contingents are annihilating.

---

1. *Tamhīdāt*, pp. 323, 325.

This is the real faith for which one is commanded in His saying, glorified be His name: 'O you who have faith, have faith' [4:136]; and there is an indication to it in His saying: 'Whosoever has faith in God, He will guide his heart' [64:11].

By such faith, the hidden polytheism in the heart is exterminated, for 'if you associate a partner with Him, your work will fail' [39:65]. From this hidden polytheism very few people are liberated, or have been [able] to purify their heart from it [as He says]: 'And most of them believe not in God except that they associate partner with Him' [12:106]. O my brother, so long you are with thee how can it be possible for thee to have patience by God, in God and with God? If you rely upon Him [427] then He is sufficient for thee, and He is the best reliance.'

Know that the seekers of the reality seek the reality by the reality, and they find Him; the seekers of caprice seek Him by caprice and they do not find Him, and they will never find Him, for besides the reality what is there but shadows? If you do not listen to this discourse from me and do not consider it to be truthful in its significance, then listen and contemplate on what is reported from the Prophet, may peace be upon him and upon his progeny, in his saying: 'The believer takes his religion from God, the hypocrite selects an opinion and takes his religion from it',[1] and His saying: 'Haven't you seen the one who takes caprice as His god?' [28:50]; and His saying: 'Be the worshippers of God' [3:79].

Truly, the believers in reality, those who are pious, the worshippers, those sincere to God, to His Messenger and to those who hold authority from among them [Qur'ān, 4:59] are the divine sages, the worshippers of the Lord, who do not crave for this worldly [things]. Other than them are the worshippers of caprice, the worshippers of icons, the friends of idols and the forms of bodies, the companions of the graves and inhabitants of the evanescent world. 'But those who do wrong, will learn [a lesson], i.e. the Overturner will overturn

1. *Ibid.*, p. 319.

them.' May God give us and our brothers wherever they are refuge from being deluded by futile forms, from the external [or worldly] traces, from leaning to the levels of those veiled [from God], from the way-stations of evil ones, from those hidden by the hidden limitations, from the covering of scepticism and doubt, and from those turned away from the covering which conceals the 'bright destination' (*al-maḥajjat al-bayḍā*).

This is the end of what we intended to express and attempted to make evident.

Glossary

ahl al-ḥaqīqah	people of spiritual reality
al-aḥwāl	spiritual states
al-ajsām	corporeal bodies
al-anwār al-jawharīyya wa al-araḍīyya	substantial and accidental lights
al-'aql al-'amalī	practical intellect
al-'aql bi'l-malakah	intellect *in habitus*
al-'aql bi'l-fi'l intellect	in act
al-'aql al-fa''āl Active	Intellect
al-'aql al-hayūlānī	material or hylic intellect
al-'aql al-ijmālī	non-differentiated intellect
al-'aql al-kullī	Universal Intellect
al-'aql al-mustafād	acquired intellect
al-'aql al-naẓarī	theoretical intellect
al-'araḍ	accident
arbāb al-adhwāq	the people of spiritual tastes
aṣḥāb al-kalām	dialectical theologians
aṣḥāb al-mukāshifāt	the possessors of unveilings
asrār	'mysteries' (singular, *sirr*) or the level of the being of man that is higher than the 'spirit'
al-'aynīyya	concrete
al-a'yān al-thābitah	permanent archetypes

al-awṣiyā	inheritors
ʿālam al-arwāḥ	the world of spirits
ʿālam al-ashbāh	the world of apparitions or shadows
ʿāqil	intellecting
barāzikh	corporeal bodies, lit. isthmuses
basiṭah	simple
al-basharīyya	human condition
baṭin wujūd	inner being
burhān	demonstrative proof
ḍarūrat azalīyya	pre-eternal necessity
ḍarūrat dhātīyya	essential necessity
*ḍaw*light ray	
dhāt	essence
al-dhāt al-aḥadīyya	the absolute Oneness of Essence
al-dhawāt al-maʿlūlāt	the essences of the caused ones
faṣl differentia	
al-fayḍ al-aqdas	the most holy emanation
al-fayḍ al-ilāhī	divine emanation
al-fayḍ al-muqaddas	the holy emanation
fikr	cogitation
fiṭrah	primordial nature
al-futuwwah	spiritual chivalry
al-ghaḍab	irascibility
al-ghanī	self-sufficient
al-ḥads	intuitive power
al-ḥaqīqah al-Muḥamadīyya	Muhammadan reality
al-ḥaqq	reality
hay'at	modes
hayākil	temples
al-ḥijāb	veil
huwīyya	ipseity, ego
al-huwīyya al-aḥadīyya	the Oneness of Ipseity
al-huwīyyāt	ipseities
ʿibādāt	services, worships
al-ibdāʿiyyāt	originations

al-ikhtirāʿiyyāt	inventions
al-ilāhiyyūn	theosophists
al-ʿilal al-dhātīyya	the essential causes
al-ilhām	inspiration
al-ʿināyah	providence
innīyya	I-ness
al-ʿirfān	gnosis, knowledge
ishrāq	illumination
al-Ishrāqiyyūn	Illuminationist philosophers
al-islām	surrender
al-ishtirāq	equivocal
iʿitibārī	mentally posited
al-jaʿl al-basiṭ al-ibdāʿī	simple originated making
jabarūt	the world of intellect according to Ṣadrā (lit. omnipotence)
jāʿil	maker
jins	genus
al-kāʾināt	creations
al-khafāʾ	hiddenness
khalīfah	vicegerent
al-lawḥ al-maḥfūẓ	the Preserved Tablet
māhīyya	essence or reality
al-māhiyyāt	quiddities
al-maʿād	the Return
al-maʿārif	gnosis
maʿqūl	intelligible
al-majdhubūn	ecstatics
al-malak al-muqaddas	holy angel
al-Malakūt	the immaterial world, the world of Soul
al-maqāmāt	spiritual stations
maʿrifah	gnosis
marmuzāt	symbolic tales, writings
mathal	symbol, similitude
al-maẓāhir	loci of manifestation
maẓhar	locus of manifestation

al-mizāj	temperament
al-muʿāmilāt	transactions
munawwir	one who illuminates
al-mushāhidah al-ḥuḍurīyya	the witnessing by presence
al-mushāhidāt	spiritual visions
muslim	surrendered
al-mutajallā	epiphanizes, self-manifests
al-muwaḥḥidūn	men of unification
al-nafs	soul
al-nafs al-kullīyya	Universal Soul
al-nafs al-nabātī	vegetal soul
al-nafs al-nāṭiqah	rational soul
al-nafs al-nāṭiqah al-malakīyya	angelic rational soul
al-nafas al-raḥmānī	the Breath of Mercifulness
al-nash'at	mode of existence
al-nash'at al-dā'imah	the eternal mode of existence
al-nash'at al-ukhrā	the next mode of existence
al-nufūs al-ḥissiyya	sentient souls
al-nufūs al-khayāliyya	imaginative souls
al-nufūs al-wahmānīyya	estimative souls
al-nūr al-anwār	the Light of lights
al-nūr al-ḥaqq	the light of the reality
al-nūr al-ilāhī	divine Light
al-nūr al-maḥsūs	sensible light
al-nūr al-maḥsūs al-āriḍ	accidental sensible light
nūr Muḥammad	the light of Muhammad
al-nūr al-mumkin	contingent light
al-nūr al-qayyūmī	self-subsisting light
nurīyya	luminosity
al-qaḍā'	Decree, or universal forms of things in the Intellect.
al-qadar	Allotment, or particular forms of things in the Soul.
al-qaḍā' al-ijmālī	non-differentiated Decree

al-qawābil	receptacles or recipients
qayyūmīyya	self-subsistence
al-quwwah	faculty
al-quwwah al-fikrīyya wa'l-fikr	cogitative and reflective faculty
al-quwwah al-mutaṣarrifah	the governing faculty or the faculty of disposal
al-ru'yā'	vision, dream
al-rūḥ al-ḥaywānī	animal spirit
al-rūḥ al-nafsānī	pneumatic spirit
al-rūḥ al-ṭabī'ī	natural spirit
al-sālikūn	wayfarers
al-shafā'ah	intercession
al-shahwah	appetite
al-shar' al-anwar	the most luminous divine Law
sharī'ah	divine Law, direct course
al-shuhūd	spiritual witnessing
ṣudūr	generation
al-ṣūfī	purifier
ṣuwar al-naw'īyya	specific forms
ta'ayyun	determined or fixed state
ta'ayyunāt	determinations
tajallā	theophanized or self-manifested
tajalliyyāt	theophanies
tajarrud	disengagement
takawwun	generation
al-takhyil	imagination
al-tamthīlāt,	conceptualizations, lit. 'imaginalizations'
al-taqlīd	unreflective imitation
al-taqwā	piety
taṣarruf	disposal, governing
al-taṣawwuf	purification
al-tashbihāt	metaphors
al-tashkīk	analogical gradation

al-'ulūm al-'aqlīyya	intellectual sciences
umm al-kitāb	the essence of the Book
walāyah	friendship
walī	friend
al-wujūd	existence
wujūd al-wujudāt	the Being of beings or the Existence of existences
ẓāhiriyyūn	externalists
ẓalāl mamdūdah	extended shadows
al-zuhd	ascetic practice
al-ẓuhūr	manifestation
al-ẓulmah	darkness

Bibliography

Abdūh, M. (Commentator) *Nahj al-Balāghah*. Beirut: Dār al-ma'rifah, n.d.

Ayoub, M. 'The Speaking Qur'ān and the Silent Qur'ān: A Study of the Principles and Developments of Imāmī Shiī'ī *tafsīr*', in A. Rippin (ed.) *Approaches to the History of the Interpretation of the Qur'ān*. Oxford: Clarendon, 1988.

Chittick, W. C. *The Sufi Path of Knowledge*. Albany: State University of New York, 1989.

Cleary, T. *Living and Dying with Grace: Counsels of Ḥaḍrat 'Alī*. Boston: Shambhala, 1996.

Corbin, H. *En Islam iranien*, vols I and IV. Paris: Gallimard, 1972.

Furūzānfar, Badī' al-Zamān. *Aḥādīth-i Mathnawī*. Tehran: Amīr Kabīr, 1347/1967.

Al-Ghazzālī, Abū Ḥāmid. *Al-Mishkāt al-Anwār*, translated by D. Buchman as *The Niche of Lights*. Provo, Utah: Brigham Young University Press, 1998.

—— *Iḥyā' al-'ulūm al-Dīn*. Cairo, n.d.

Hamadānī, 'Ayn al-Quḍḍāt. *Tamhīdāt*. Tehran: Intishārāt Minūchehr, n.d.

Ibn al-'Arabī. *Al-Futūḥāt al-Makkīyya*. Cairo, 1911; (reprint) Beirut: Dār al-Ṣādir, n.d.

Isfahānī Ḥ. N. (ed.) *The Complete Philosophical Treatises of Ṣadr al-Dīn Muḥammad al-Shīrāzī*. Tehran: Hekmat Publishing, 1999.

Izutsu, T. *The Concept and Reality of Existence*. Tokyo: Keio University, 1971.
—— *Sufism and Taoism*. Berkeley: University of California Press, 1983.
—— 'Mysticism and the Linguistic Problem of Equivocation in the Thought of 'Ayn al-Quḍḍāt Hamadānī', in his *Creation and the Timeless Order of Things*. Ashland, Oregon: White Cloud Press, 1994.
Khan, M. M. (translator) *Ṣaḥīḥ al-Bukhārī*, vol. 1, Arabic text with English translation. Delhi: Kitab Bhavan, 1987.
Kulaynī, Shaykh Muḥammad bin Ya'qūb. *Uṣūl al-Kāfī*, edited with Persian translation and commentary by Jawād Muṣtafā, Shiraz: 'Ilmīyeh Islāmī, 1344 A.H./1385 H.S.
Kusnipur, B. 'Perception: A Way to Perfection in Sadra', in *Transcendent Philosophy*, vol. 1:2, pp. 41–62.
Marmura. M. E. (translator) 'Avicenna: On the Proof of Prophecies', in *Medieval Political Philosophy*, edited by R. Lerner and M. Mahdi. New York: Cornell University Press, third edition, 1983.
Nasr, S. H. *The Islamic Intellectual Tradition in Persia*, edited by M. A. Razavi. Richmond, Surrey: Curzon Press, 1996.
—— 'Mullā Ṣadrā and the Doctrine of Unity of Being', in *Islamic Life and Thought*. London: George Allen & Unwin, 1981.
—— 'Mullā Ṣadrā as a Source for the History of Islamic Philosophy', in *Islamic Life and Thought*. London: George Allen & Unwin, 1981.
—— 'Mullā Ṣadrā: His Teaching', chapter 36, pp. 643–661 in *History of Islamic Philosophy*, part 1, edited by S. H. Nasr and O. Leaman. London: Routledge, 1996.
—— 'The Polarization of Being', in *Islamic Life and Thought*. London: George Allen & Unwin, 1981.
—— 'Qur'ānic Commentaries of Mullā Ṣadrā', in *Consciousness and Reality: Studies in Memory of Toshihiko Izutsu*, edited by S. J. Āshtiyānī and others. Tokyo: Iwanami Shoten, 1998.
—— *Ṣadr al-Dīn Shīrāzī and his Transcendent Theosophy*. Tehran: Institute for Humanities and Cultural Studies, 1997.

Nurbakhsh, J. *Traditions of the Prophet.* New York: Khanqahi-Nimatullahi, 1981.

Peerwani, L. 'Mullā Ṣadrā on Imaginative Perception and Imaginal World', in *Transcendent Philosophy*, vol. 1:2, pp. 81–96.

—— 'Mullā Ṣadrā on the Theory of Causal Efficacy', forthcoming in the Proceedings of the 2nd International Conference on Mulla Sadra held at S.O.A.S., London, in 2001.

—— 'Qur'ānic Hermeneutic: The View of Ṣadr al-Dīn Shīrāzī' in *BRISMES Proceedings*, 1991, pp. 468–477.

—— 'Reincarnation or Resurrection of the Soul? Mullā Ṣadrā's Philosophical Solution to the Dilemma', in *Transcendent Philosophy*, vol. 3:2, pp. 115–130.

Al-Qummī, Abū'l-Ḥasan Ibrāhim. *Tasfsīr al-Qummī.* Beirut: Dār al-Surūr, 1991.

Rhaman, Fazlur. *The Philosophy of Mullā Ṣadrā.* Albany: State University of New York, 1975.

Rubin, U. 'Pre-existence and Light: Aspects of the Concept of Nūr Muḥammad', in *Islamic Oriental Studies*, vol. V, 1995, pp. 62–119.

Ṣadrā Mullā (Ṣadr al-Dīn Muḥammad ibn Ibrāhim al-Shīrāzī). *'Arshīyya.* Translated by J. Morris as *Wisdom of the Throne.* Princeton: Princeton University, 1981.

—— *Asfār al-Ḥikmat al-Muta'āliyah fī al-Asfār al-Arba'ah*, 9 volumes. Beirut: Dār Iḥyā al-Turāth al-Arabī, 1981.

—— *Asrār al-Āyāt*, translated into Persian by M. Khājawī. Tehran: Muṭāle'āt wa Taḥqīqāt-e Farhangī, 1406/1985.

—— *Kasr Aṣnām al-Jāhilīyya*, edited by M. T. Dāneshpazhuh. Tehran: Maṭba' Jāme'-ye Tehran, 1962.

—— *Mafātiḥ al-Ghayb*, edited by M. Khājawī. Tehran: Mu'assese-ye Muṭāle'āt wa Taḥqīqāt-e Farhangī, 1406/1985.

—— *Majmu-i Ash'ār*, edited by M. Khājawī. Tehran: Mawlā publication, 1386/1988

—— *'Al-Mutashābihāt al-Qur'ān'*, in *Rasā'il Falsafī* of Ṣadr al-Dīn al-Shīrāzī, edited by S. J. Āshtiyānī. Mashhad: Daneshgāhe Mashhad, 1392/1972.

—— *Se Aṣl*, edited by S. H. Nasr. Tehran: Dāneshghāhe Tehran, 1380/1960.

—— *Sharḥ Uṣūl al-Kāfī: Kitāb al-'aql wa al-Jahl*, edited by M. Khājawī. Tehran: Mu'assese-ye Muṭāle 'āt wa Taḥqīqāt-e Farhangī, 1409/1986.

—— *Tafsīr al-Qur'ān al-Karīm*, 7 volumes, edited by M. Khājawī. Qum: Intishārāt-e Bīdār, 1409/1986.

Al-Suhrawardī, Shihāb al-Dīn. *Kitāb Ḥikmat al-Ishrāq*, translated by J. Walbridge and H. Ziai as *The Philosophy of Illumination*. Provo, Utah: Brigham Young University Press, 1999.

Al-Tirmidhī. *Al-Jāmi' al-Ṣaḥīḥ wa huwa Sunan al-Tirmidhi*, edited by A. M. Shākir. Cairo: al-Maktabat al-Islāmīyya, 1938.

Al-Ṭūsī, Naṣīr al-Dīn. *Sharḥ al-Ishārāt wa al-Tanbīhāt*. Tehran, 1378/1958.

Ricoeur, P. *The Conflict of Interpretations*. Evanston: North Western University Press, 1974.

Ṭabāṭabā'ī, 'Allāmah Sayyid M. H. *The Qur'ān in Islam*. London: Zahra Publications, 1987.

Wolfson, H. A. *The Philosophy of the Kalam*, Cambridge: Harvard University Press, 1976

Al-Zamakhsharī. *Al-Kashshāf*, Vol. 3. Beirut: Dār al-'Ālamīyya, n.d.

Ziai, H. *Knowledge and Illumination*. Providence: Brown University, 1990.

Index of the Qur'ānic Verses

2:31–32	And He taught Adam all the names, then showed them to the angels … 390
2:34	Prostrate yourselves to Man (Adam). 410, 412
2:257	God is the Friend (*walī*) of those who believe … 361, 362, 362
3:7	Its ultimate *ta'wīl* is known to God alone. [Trans. introduction, section B]
3:18	There is no god but Him. 426
3:18	God bears witness, and so do the angels and all who are endowed with knowledge … 426
3:79	Be the worshippers of the Lord. 385, 420
3:133	And be quick for forgiveness from your Lord. 408
3:164	Certainly God conferred a benefit upon the believers when He raised … 366
3:185	The life of this world is nothing but an enjoyment of self-delusion. 424
3:190	In the changing of day to night there are signs … [Trans. Introduction, sect. D)
4:80	So he who obeys the Messenger has obeyed God. 387
4:113	He has taught thee what thou knewest not. 407
4:136	O you who have faith, have faith. 426

4:174	We have sent down to you a clear light. 350
5:15	There has come to you from God a light, and a manifest Book. 419
6:59	With Him are the keys of the Invisible; none but He knows them. 406
6:75	Thus did We show Abraham the kingdom of the heavens ... 54
6:76	I love not the setters. 525
6:79	I have turned my face to Him who originated the heavens and the earth ... 416
6:103	The sights perceive Him not, but He perceives the sights. 386, 421
6:162	My prayer and my sacrifice and my living and my dying are for God ... 425
7:54	Verily His are the creation and command. 410
7:54	Surely your Lord is God Who created the heavens and the earth in six days ... 420
7:143	And when His Lord self-manifested Himself to the mountain He made it ... 388
7:154	He took up the tablets, and in their inscription there was guidance. 407
8:5	It is not up to a human that God ... [Trans. Introduction, sec. B)
8:17	You did not throw when you threw but God threw. 367
9:78	God is the great Knower of the invisible things. 360
9:111	God has bought from the believers their souls and their possessions ... 387
12:106	And most of them believe not in God except that they associate partner with Him. 426
12:108	Say: this is my path: I call to God upon insight, I and whosoever follows me. 407
13:4	Watered with the same water, yet We make some of them ... 413

13:39	God obliterates what He wills, and He establishes [what He wills], and with Him … 396
15:22	We cause the rain to descend from the sky. 413
15:29	When I have fashioned him [in due proportion] and blew unto him My spirit … 387, 412
15:99	Worship thy Lord until the certainty comes to thee. 419
16:40	I say to a thing: Be, and it is. 366
17:1	Glory be to Him Who carried His servant by night from the Inviolable Mosque … 378, 397
17:13–14	And every man's acts [*ṭā'ir*, lit. bird] have We fastened to his neck … 396
17:21	Surely the next world is greater in levels, and greater in preferment. 424
18:65	And We taught him knowledge from Us. 418
19:95	All of them come alone on the Day of Resurrection. 363
20:5	The All-Merciful sat upon the Throne. 379
20:10	I observe a fire. 378
20:111	They cannot encompass Him by knowledge, all faces are humbled unto Him … 421
21:104	As We originated the first creation, so shall We bring it back. 393, 397
21:104	On the Day when We shall roll up heaven as a scroll is rolled up … 397
21:107	We have not sent thee save as a mercy unto all worlds. 419
23:14	So blessed be God, the best of creators. 410
23:20	… a tree springing out from the Mount Sinai, that produces oil … 373
24:35	God guides to His light whom He wills. 379
24:63	Deem not the call of the Messenger among yourselves like the call of you … 384
25:43	Have you seen him who has taken his caprice to be his god? 425

25:45	Have you not seen how thy Lord has spread the shadow? 388
26:90–91	For the righteous, the Garden is brought near to them, and for those straying … 413
27:82	And when the Word is fulfilled against them, We shall bring forth for them … 415
28:50	Haven't you seen the one who takes his caprice as his god? 427
28:56	Surely you cannot guide whom you love. 367
31:20	He has lavished on you His blessings, externally and internally. 409
31:164	Certainly God conferred a benefit upon the believers. 366
32:5	His Command governs the affair from the heaven to the earth. 1360, 385
33:6	The Prophet is nearer to those who have faith than their own souls. 401
33:72	We did indeed offer the Trust to the heavens, the earth and the mountains … 367, 387, 387
34:54	Between them and what they desire is placed a barrier. 414
35:34	Praise be to God Who has put grief away from us … 417
37:99	I am going to my Lord Who will guide me right. 378
39:22	Is he whose breast God has opened up to submission (*islām*), so that he follows … 351
39:54	So turn ye to your Lord. 408
39:65	If you associate a partner with Him, your work will fail. 426
41:31	Therein shall you have what your souls desire. 412
41:40	Is he who is cast into the Fire better, or he who comes safe through … 398
41:44	They call from a far place. 413

41:53	We shall show them Our signs upon the horizons and in themselves ... 386, 406
41:54	Are they still in doubt about the meeting with their Lord? 386
42:53	Unto God all things come home. 367
43:71	Therein shall be all the objects of the souls' appetite, and the eyes delight. 413
45:13	And He has subjected to you what is in the heavens ... 409, 410
48:26	And [Allah] bound them to the word of piety and well were they ... 387
50:30	Are you filled? And it replies: Are there any more [to come]? 375
51:21	And in yourselves, do you not see? 387, 406
51:49	Of everything We have created pairs. 362
51:56	I created the jinn and humankind only that they serve Me. 386
52:3	... a fine parchment unrolled. 407
52:4–6	And the House frequented, and the roof uplifted and the sea swarming. 407, 410
53:1–5	By the star when it falls, your comrade is not astray, nor is he deceived ... 388
53:10–11	Then He revealed to His servant that which He revealed. The heart lied not ... 388, 390
53:42–43	The final end is unto thy Lord, and that He it is Who makes one to laugh ... 426
55:29	Each day He is upon some task. 395
56:79	Only the pure ones can touch it. [Transl. Introduction, sec. D]
59:7	So take what the Messenger gives you. 407
62:6	Ye who are Jews, if you claim that you are the friends of God apart from ... 417
64:11	Whosoever has faith in God, He will guide his heart. 426
66:8	Their light running before them, and on their right hands. 425

66:8	Our Lord, perfect our light for us. 425
67:10	Had we but listened and intellected [or reflected] we would not have been ... 422
73:1	O thou enwrapped in thy robes. 419
74:30	Are nineteen above it. 375
75:22–23	Some faces on that day shall be radiant, gazing at their Sustainer. 366
78:2–3	The awesome tidings concerning which they are in disagreement. 407
79:46	On the day they behold it, it will be as if they have tarried for an evening ... 425
82:16	And they will not be absent from them. 413
83:7	Surely the book of vile is in the *Sijjīn*. 398
83:15	Verily that day they shall be veiled from their Lord. 414
83:18	And verily the book of the righteous is in the *'Illiyyūn*. 398
83:19–21	And what does convey unto you what *'Illiyyūn* is! A written book ... 397
89:30	Thou enter among My servants and enter in my Garden. 413
93:6	Did He not find thee an orphan and gave thee shelter? 419
96:3–5	Recite and your Lord is the Most Bounteous, Who taught by the pen ... 369
96:14	Does he not know that God sees? 386
103:2–3	Surely man is in a state of loss, save those who believe, and do righteous deeds. 387
104:7	The Fire of God [kindled] to a blaze that rises up to the hearts. 414
112:1	He is God, the One. 364

Index of Ḥadīths and Sayings

Abandonment of the world makes the soul happy … (Ṣūfī saying) 424
The believer takes his religion from God … 427
By God! God self-discloses to His creation … (Ja'far al-Ṣādiq) [Transl. Introduction, sec. D]
By Thee I am alive, by Thee I die. 421
The dearest thing to me is prayer. 419
The first creation that God created was the Intellect. 399
The first thing that God created was my light. 383, 398, 421
For you is this tree, use the oil of olive for the treatment of ulcers … 372
God the Exalted created the creation in darkness … 360
God the Exalted revealed to the Messenger on the night of (his) Ascension … (Ṣūfī saying) 390
God is the existence of the heavens and the earth. (Ṣūfī saying) 357
God is the source of existents. (al-Ḥallāj) 357
He will not enter the celestial heavens unless born twice. (Jesus) 424
He who dies and has not known the Imam of the time has died the death of ignorance. 401
He who has seen me has indeed seen the reality. 387, 421, 425
He who knows his soul has known his Lord. 401
He who obeys me, obeys God. 401

The hearts become rusty as iron becomes rusty. Their polish is the remembrance of God. 417
Heaven made a lot of noise and it had every reason to do so … 415
His character trait was the Qur'ān. 408
His proof is that He is God. (Ṣūfī saying) 389
Human condition is an obstacle to lordship. (Abū Yazīd Basṭāmī) 417
I am more aware of the states of heavens … ('Alī) 415
I am not like anyone among you for I stayed in the house with my Lord… 373, 384, 388
I do not see anything but God in it … ('Alī) [Transl. Introduction, sec. D]
I did not look at a thing save I saw God in it. ('Alī) 388
I saw Him in the imaginalForm. 421
I saw Him then I worshipped Him … ('Alī) 421
I saw my Lord in His I-ness and reality. 421
I saw my Lord by my Lord … (Dhu'l Nūn Miṣrī) 421
I saw my Lord in a dream in the form of my mother. (Ṣūfī saying) 416
I was a hidden treasure … 386, 387
I would not have worshipped a Lord whom I had not seen. ('Alī) 357–358
If anyone desires to look at a walking dead then let him look at me. 408
If Moses had been in my time he would have to follow me. 383
If not for you, I would not have created the spheres. 386
If this tree was in the world then either it would pertain to the Orient … (Ḥasan al-Baṣrī) 370
If the world before God weighed the measure of the wings of a mosquito … 414, 424
If you become free then you become a servant. (Ṣūfī saying) 366
In the Garden there is none but God the Exalted. (Shiblī) 357
Indeed God created Adam in the image of the Most Merciful. 383
Indeed God created my light from the light of His Might. 384
Indeed God does not look at your forms and your deeds but He looks at your hearts … 386

It was a light that I saw. 352, 420
It is that Light which when kindles in the heart … 351
It is prepared for my virtuous servants what no eye has seen … 413
Kill 'me' O my trustworthy friends … (al-Ḥallāj) 417
Knowledge is a veil. (Ṣūfī saying) [Transl. Introduction, sec. D)
(The Light) is He Who gives forms to things … (Ṣūfī saying) 361
(The Light) is He Who guides the hearts toward the traces of the reality … (Ṣūfī saying) 361
(The Light) is He Who illumines the hearts of the gnostics by His unity … (Ṣūfī saying) 361
The mark of a disciple in the [state of] annihilation … (Abū Sa'īd al-Kharrāz) 367
Me and the guardian of orphan are like these two [fingers] in the Garden. 419
My heart saw my Lord. ('Alī) 388
My Lord taught me courtesy, so how beautiful has been … 387
None can see my Lord save my Lord. (al-Ḥallāj) 421
O God, grant me light in my heart, light in my hearing… 425–426
O the Light of lights! O the Manager … 426
O my God, what is the wisdom in my creation? (Ṣūfī saying) 385
Oh! How I yearn to meet my brothers who come after me. 387
The purifier is indeed God … (Ṣūfī saying) 418
The Qur'ān has inner and outer meanings … [Trans. Introduction, sec. B]
Reflect upon the instruments of God; reflect not upon God's Essence. 421
The servant's life must be like the life of his Lord. (Uways Qaranī) 366
Servitude without lordship is deficiency and evanescence … (Ṣūfī saying) 387
The similitude of me and the similitude of [my being in] the world … 419
The similitude of the heart is like the mirror, when a man looks into it his Lord …414
There is a market in the Garden [or Paradise] in which the forms are bought. 416

There is no good in a tree on which the sun never shines... 372
There is no good in any worship if there is no understanding ... ('Alī) [Transl. Introduction, sec. D]
There is no peace for the believers without meeting God. 358
There is no verse of the Qur'ān that does not possess exoteric ... ('Alī) [Transl. Introduction, sec. B]
There is none in the two worlds but my Lord... (Abū'l-'Abbās) 357
They recite the Qur'ān but it does not transcend their throats. [Transl. Introduction, sec. D]
This world is a corpse, its seekers are dogs. 419
You are the manifest book by whose signs what is hidden in it manifests ... ('Alī) 391
The vilest of mankind is the one whose [life is geared] to eating only. 422
We heard from Khiḍr...God created the light of Muhammad ... (Sahl al-Tustarī) 384
What has dust to do with the Lord of lords. (Arabic proverb) 387
What is the measure of the world compared with the next world ... 424
Whatever is in the heavens and the earth ... asks for atonement of the learned. 409
Woe to him who recites the Qur'ān but does not reflect upon it. [Transl. Introduction, sec. D]
Whoever makes the commentary on the Qur'ān according to his own opinion ... [Transl. Introduction, sec. B]
(The world) is a house for the one who has no house. 419

Index of Names

'Abd'allāh ibn Mas'ūd 40
Abū'l-'Abbās 49
ahl al-bayt (people of the house)
ahl al-ḥaqīqah (people of spiritual reality)
Aḥmad ibn Ḥanbal 19
al-aḥwāl (spiritual states) 41
al-ajsām (corporeal bodies) 43
Allāhwirdī Khān 10
'Alī ibn Abī Ṭālib ; Commander of the Faithful 15, 18, 24, 25, 49, 89, 92, 95, 125, 132
accident (*al-'araḍ*); accidents 35
arbāb al-adhwāq (people of spiritual tastes) 41
Aristotle 55, 98
aṣḥāb al-kalām (*kalām* or dialectical theologians) 35,
aṣḥāb al-mukāshifāt (companions of unveilings) 41
asrār (mysteries, singular, *sirr*) or the level of the being of man which is higher than the 'spirit'
Asrār al-āyāt 11
Attributes (divine): of Beauty; of Majesty 24, 55, 56, 60, 61, 71, 77, 96, 99, 100, 107, 109
Avicenna (Ibn Sina) 31, 80, 149?
al-'aynīyah (concrete) 98
al-a'yān al-thābitah (permanent archetypes) 50
al-awṣiyā (Inheritors) 115

barāzikh (corporeal bodies), lit. isthmuses 45
basiṭah (simple) 36
al-basharīyah (human condition) 116
being or existence (*wujūd*): Absolute Existence or Being; contingent; inner being (*bāṭin wujūd*); 41, 43
The breath of the Mercifulness (*al-nafas al-raḥmānī*) 45
burhān (demonstrative proof) 43

ḍarūrat azalīyah (pre-eternal necessity) 44
ḍarūrat dhātīyah (essential necessity) 44
Day of Resurrection; the Last Day; 57, 62, 102, 103, 104
ḍaw' (light-ray) 45
Diḥyā al-Kalbī 126
divine Speech; divine Word 14
Dualists 55
Dhū'l-Nūn al-Misrī

epiphany; epiphanized 29, 41, 61, 102, 104
essence (*dhāt*): the absolute Oneness of Essence (*al-dhāt al-aḥadīyah*); the essences of the caused ones (*al-dhawāt al-ma'lūlāt*); Divine Essence 44, 60, 78

Face of God 59, 124
faculty (*al-quwwah*); cogitative and reflective faculty (*al-quwwah al-fikrīyah wa'l-fikr*); of disposal or of governing (*al-quwwah al-mutaṣarrifah*) 73–77
faṣl (differentia) 47, 80, 94
al-fayḍ al-aqdas (the most holy emanation); *al-fayḍ al-ilāhī* (divine emanation); *al-fayḍ al-muqaddas* (the holy emanation) 39, 45
fikr (cogitation) 40
fiṭrah (primordial nature) 85
al-futuwwah (spiritual chivalry) 33

Gabriel (angel) 126
Garden (Paradise) 49, 63, 69, 72, 90, 116, 118, 121-124, 126, 131, 156, 160, 161
al-ghaḍab (irascibility) 41
al-ghanī (self-sufficient) 43
Ghazzālī, Abū Ḥāmid 31, 37, 149
gnosis (*'irfān*); gnostics (*'urafā'*) 10, 29, 74

al-ḥads (intuitive power) 81
al-Hallāj [Manṣūr] 49
al-ḥaqq (Reality) 23, 37, 38
Ḥasan al-Baṣrī 28, 69, 160
hay'at (modes) 43
hayākil (temples) 45
Hell; hell-Fire; Fire 54, 56, 75, 107, 116, 121, 122
al-Ḥikmat al-muta'ālīyah (Transcendent Theosophy) 96

huwīyah ipseity, ego; *al-huwīyah al-aḥadīyah* (the Onensess of Ipseity); *al-huwīyāt* (ipseities) 35, 48, 61, 127

'ibādāt (services, worships) 62
ibdā'iyāt (originations) 109
Ibn 'Abbās 18, 27, 133
Ibn Mas'ūd 124
Ibrāhim Shīrāzī (Mullā Ṣadrā's father) 9
ikhtirā'iyāt (inventions) 109
ilāhiyūn (theosophists) 106
al-'ilal al-dhātīyah (the essential causes) 78
ilhām (inspiration) 41
illumination (*ishrāq*) 23, 26, 29, 32, 38, 40, 53, 54, 61, 73, 82, 83, 96, 113
'ināyah (providence) 77
innīyah (I-ness) 48
intellect (*'aql*): practical intellect (*al-'aql al-'amalī*); intellect in *habitus* (*al-'aql bi'l-malakah*); intellect in act (*al-'aql bi'l-fa'al*); Active Intellect (*al-'aql al-fa''āl*); material or hylic intellect (*al-'aql al-hayūlānī*); non-differentiated intellect (*al-'aql al-ijmālī*); Universal Intellect (*al-'aql al-kullī*); acquired intellect (*al-'aql al-mustafād*); theoretical intellect (*al-'aql al-naẓarī*); intelligible (*ma'qūl*) 18, 65, 66, 70, 74, 77, 82, 111
intercession (*shafā'at*) 62, 104
islām (surrender) 40
ishtirāq (equivocal) 35
al-Ishārāt [*wa*] *al-tanbīhāt* 152
i'itibārī (mentally posited) 49

al-jā'al al-basiṭ al-ibdā'ī (simple originated making) 44
Jabarūt (the world of Intellect according to Ṣadrā (lit. Omnipotence) 56
jā'il (maker) 48

jins (genus) 36

kashf (spiritual unveiling) 23, 25
al-Kashshāf 38
al-Kāfī (*uṣūl*) 105, 150, 152
al-kā'ināt (creations) 109
Ka'b al-Aḥbār 51
al-khafā' (hiddenness) 36
Khālidāt islands 71
al-Kharrāz, Abū Sa'yīd 64, 161
Khalīl (prophet Abraham) 77, 127
al-Kulaynī, Shaykh Muḥammad bin Ya'qūb 105
Kumayl ibn Ziyād 89

al-lawḥ al-maḥfūẓ the Preserved Tablet 70
light (*nūr*): accidental sensible (*al-nūr al-maḥsūs al-āriḍ*); contingent (*al-nūr al-mumkin*); Divine Light (*al-nūr al-ilāhī*); the Light of lights (*al-nūr al-anwār*); of Existence; of Muhammad (*nūr Muḥammad*) or Muḥammadan light; of the Reality (*al-nūr al-ḥaqq*); self-subsisting (*al-nūr al-qayyūmī*); sensible (*al-nūr al-maḥsūs*); luminosity (*nurīyah*) 12, 31, 33, 35, 36, 38, 42-44, 52, 59, 85, 113

Mafātiḥ al-ghayb 11
māhīyah (quiddity; essence or reality); quiddities (*al-māhiyāt*) 35, 94
al-ma'ād (the Return) 74
al-ma'ārif (gnosis) 129
al-majdhubūn (ecstatics) 40
al-malak al-muqaddas (holy angel) 66
al-Malakūt (the non-material world, the world of Soul) 74
maqāmāt (spiritual stations) 41
ma'rifah (gnosis) 89
marmuzāt (symbolic tales, writings) 37
mathal (symbol, similitude) 39, 59,
maẓhar (locus of manifestation); *maẓāhir* (loci of manifestation) 37, 39
mi'rāj (ascent) 42
Mīr Dāmād 9
Mīr Findiriskī 9
al-Mīzān 30
Mishkāt al-anwār 31
Moses 72, 78, 84, 91, 127, 160
al-mu'āmilāt (transactions) 41
Mujāhid ibn Jabr 18
Mullā 'Abd al-Razzāq Lāhijī 10
Mullā Muḥsin Fayḍ Kāshānī 10
Munawwir (one who illuminates) 35
Munkar and Nakīr (the angels) 117
Muqātil ibn Sulaymān 18
al-mushāhadah al-ḥuḍurīyah (the witnessing by presence) 52
muslim surrendered 127, 128
al-mutajallā (epiphanized, self-manifested) 45
Mutashābihāt al-Qur'ān 11, 151
al-muwaḥḥidūn men of unification 95

nafs, see soul 23, (41), 73, 79, 129, 130, 138
Najm al-Dīn (Dāyāh Rāzī) 93
al-nash'at (mode of existence); *al-nash'at al-dā'imah* (the eternal mode of existence); *al-nash'at al-ukhrā* (the next mode of existence) 72, 107
Nasr, Seyyed Hossein 7, 32, 150, 151
nūr, see light 12, 32, 31, 33, 35, 36, 38, 42-44, 52, 59, 85, 113

Perfect Man 32, 94, 95, 102, 104, 105, 107, 113, 115, 121
Philosophers: Illuminationist; Peripatetic 31, 36, 37, 42, 43, 44, 53
Plato; Platonic Ideas 29, 120
Plotinus 29
Prophet (Muḥammad); Messenger (of God) 9, 10, 14, 15, 31, 33, 49, 59, 62-

64, 71, 78, 84, 86, 87, 90-92, 94, 104, 107, 108, 125-129, 132, 133, 141, 151, 156

al-qaḍā' (Decree, or universal forms of things in the Intellect); non-differentiated Decree (*al-qaḍā' al-ijmālī*) 68, 111
al-qadar (Allotment, or particular forms of things in the Soul) 68
Qatādah 28
al-qawābil (receptacles, or recipients) 37
qayyūmīyah (self-subsistence) 51
al-Qummī 29

Rāzī, Fakhr al-Dīn 29
Reality (*al-ḥaqq*). 23, 24, 25, 37, 38, 39, 40, 46, 49, 51, 52, 54, 55, 60, 61, 62, 64, 82, 83, 86, 88, 89, 90, 92, 94, 104, 105, 106, 108, 114, 115, 116, 123, 129, 130, 133, 137, 139, 140, 141, 150, 159, 161
Resurrection 20, 58, 62, 102-104, 151, 155
Ricoeur, P. 16, 152
rūḥ, see spirit 41, 65, 73
al-ru'yā' (vision, dream) 42

Satan (*iblis*) 52, 55, 85, 116
Ṣālih, Muḥsin 32
Shām (the present day Palestine, Jordan and Syria) 71
al-Shiblī 49
Socrates 29
soul (*nafs*): angelic rational soul (*al-nafs al-nāṭiqah al-malakīyah*); rational (*al-nafs al-nāṭiqah*); Universal Soul (*al-nafs al-kullīyah*); vegetal (*al-nafs al-nabātī*); estimative souls (*al-nufūs al-wahmānīyah*); imaginative souls (*al-nufūs al-khayāliyah*); sentient souls (*al-nufūs al-ḥissiyah* 66, 73, 129, 154, 156, 157, 159
spirit (*ruḥ*); animal spirit (*al-ruḥ al-ḥaywānī*); natural (*al-ruḥ al-ṭabī'ī*); psychic (*al-ruḥ al-nafsānī*) 41, 65, 73
al-salikūn (wayfarers) 40
al-shahwah (appetite) 41
sharī'ah (divine Law, direct course); *al-shar' al-anwar* (the most luminous divine Law) 75, 85, 120
Shaykh Bahā' al-Dīn Āmilī 9
spiritual unveiling (*kashf*) 21, 22, 23, 25, 29
spiritual witnessing or spiritual vision ((*al-shuhūd*); spiritual visions (*al-mushāhadāt*) substance 74
ṣudūr (generation) 61
al-ṣūfī (purifier) 129
ṣuwar al-naw'īyah (specific forms) 43

ta'ayyun (determined or fixed state); *ta'ayyunāt* (determinations) 37, 127
al-Ṭabarasī 29
Ṭabāṭabā'ī, Allāmah 30, 152
tafsīr bi'l-ra'y (commentary according to one's opinion) 18
al-Tafsīr al-kabīr 12
tajallā (self-manifestation); (*tajallī*) self-disclosure 25, 36
tajalliyāt (theophanies) 37
tajarrud (disengagement) 39
takawwun (generation) 70
al-takhyil (imagination) 76
al-tamthīlāt (imaginalizations) 126
al-taqlīd (unreflective imitation) 127
al-taqwā (piety) 90
taṣarruf (disposal, governing) 76
al-taṣawwuf (purification) 129
al-tashbihāt (metaphors) 38
al-tashkīk (analogical gradation) 43
ta'wīl (interpretation, spiritual interpretation) 15

temperament (*al-mizāj*) 110
Ṭūsī, Naṣīr al-Dīn 80
Tustarī, Sahl ibn 'Abdullāh 87, 162

al-'ulūm al-'aqlīyah (intellectual sciences) 41
umm al-kitāb (the essence of the Book) 101
Uways al-Qaranī 63

veil (*ḥijāb*, plu. *ḥujūb*, veils) 36
vicegerent (*khalīfah*) 32, 94, 105, 111, 112, 118, 119

al-Wāḥidī 40
walāyah (friendship); *walī* (friend) 38, 127, 153
al-Wasīt 40
world (*'ālam*): contingent; of apparitions or shadows (*'ālam al-ashbāḥ*); of Command; of corporeal bodies and apparitions; of Creation; of spirits (*'ālam al-arwāḥ*); 39
wujūd, see being 41, 43

ẓāhiriyūn (externalists) 125
ẓalāl mamdūdah (extended shadows) 43
Zamakhsharī 29, 152
al-zuhd (ascetic practice) 136
al-ẓuhūr (manifestation) 36
al-ẓulmah (darkness) 36

On the Hermeneutics of the Light Verse of the Qur'ān